The Rising Tides of Beru

By

Roger Bunyan

Copyright © 2023 Roger Bunyan

ISBN: 978-1-916981-16-4

All rights reserved, including the right to reproduce this book, or portions thereof in any form. No part of this text may be reproduced, transmitted, downloaded, decompiled, reverse engineered, or stored, in any form or introduced into any information storage and retrieval system, in any form or by any means, whether electronic or mechanical without the express written permission of the author.

For Fern Amina

Contents

Introduction

Part One

Chapter 1 - A Seed Is Sown

Chapter 2 - Waiting

Chapter 3 - So, Where Are We Going?

Chapter 4 - Arrival

Chapter 5 - Settling In

Chapter 6 - Teaching At Hiram Bingham High School

Chapter 7 - Dancing And The Cutting Of Karewe

Chapter 8 - A Dead Whale And An Inter-Island Ship

Chapter 9 - Large Pawed Cats, A Prince, A Flying Pig And Some Chickens

Chapter 10 - Out And About

Chapter 11 - Tarawa

Chapter 12 - Back At School

Chapter 13 - A New Maneaba And Visitors To Beru

Chapter 14 - Our Final Days On Beru

Chapter 15 - Visiting High Islands On Our Way To Aoraki

Chapter 16 - Visiting More High Islands On Our Way To Wigan

Part Two

Chapter 17 - Kiribati

Chapter 18 - The Rising Tides Of Beru

Introduction

'I am afraid because we cannot stop the rising sea. I remember at night when the tides got high, it went over the sea wall. The next morning we woke up and saw the place where we keep pigs was destroyed. I hope that the sea level will not continue to rise.'

These are the words spoken by an eight-year-old girl living on the island of Tarawa in Kiribati (pronounced *kiree-bass*). The atolls of her low-lying nation in the middle of the Pacific Ocean are under threat of being submerged by rising sea levels due to global warming.

After watching the girl in a short video clip, I was alarmed. I discovered yet more examples on the internet of people in modern-day Kiribati telling similar stories and pleading for the world to help. They were islanders of all ages: teenagers with their entire lives ahead of them; adults having their homes continually battered by the sea, the elderly who had never in all their years witnessed such high waters. I was shocked, for these were the islands where my wife Jackie and I once lived many years ago during the 1970s.

We were there working for Voluntary Service Overseas (VSO) and spent two years teaching on an atoll called Beru, part of Kiribati, or the Gilbert Islands as they were then called.

These desperate voices spurred me into action; I wanted to show some support for the people with whom we had once worked and lived. I decided to write a book about our experience as VSO teachers on a small island in the middle of the vast Pacific Ocean.

Part One of this book is about our lives on Beru, and it describes our work at the school and the many challenges we faced. Barely in our twenties, this is our story of how we coped in an environment that was completely new to us. It describes some of the islanders' traditions and culture and delves into the islands' rich history. It also outlines some of the local skills we attempted to master, such as traditional dancing, cutting *karewe* from a coconut tree, and local fishing. Some of these were successful; others were dismal failures.

There are tales of sea-sickness, dead whales, wild dogs, friendly rats and cats with huge paws, of the unforgettable colours of a Pacific dusk, of clear night skies with a myriad of stars and of islanders singing and dancing in perfect harmony. And, of course, it tells you about the pupils in the school and the islanders.

The final part of this section describes other Pacific nations to which we travelled on our return journey to the UK and compares these with our own island of Beru.

Part Two, after a huge leap through four decades, brings the scene up to the present day. It describes the new nation of Kiribati and touches upon the unique geography of these scattered islands. In addition, there is a selection of historical tales from the four island regions of this new nation. Rising sea levels threaten the very existence and future of Kiribati, and there is great concern that this Pacific nation will become one of the first victims of climate change. What can be done to halt this?

As two people who were privileged to live and work on these unique islands many years ago, we feel it will be an absolute tragedy if they cease to exist. This book is a celebration of our time there but it is also a plea for powerful institutions across the world to do more to slow down global warming. Together with the inhabitants of Kiribati, we ask for a much greater effort to try to solve one of the planet's most pressing challenges. It is a race against time – and we sincerely hope it will not be too late!

The Rising Tides of Beru is dedicated to the islands and islanders of Kiribati.

Part One

Our names are Jackie and Roger Bunyan. This is our story about living and working in a school on the island of Beru in the middle of the Pacific Ocean during the 1970s. It is about the challenges we faced, and about the remarkable culture, traditions and way of life of the islanders we lived with.

These are our memories of a unique two years of our lives, where we experienced so much and hopefully gave a little in exchange.

Chapter 1

A Seed Is Sown

'Shall we go to that talk tonight? You know, about the fella who worked in India for a couple of years.'

I wasn't sure what my girlfriend was talking about. Drizzle was falling slowly out of the North Wales' sky as we shuffled towards college, trying to avoid the puddles.

'He worked for a charity. What was it? VSO, I think.' I vaguely remembered what Jackie was referring to.

'VSO? What's that?' I asked.

'Voluntary Service Overseas. It sounds interesting. We might want to do it sometime,' came the reply.

It was good that Jackie was thinking about life after college. We had been a couple for more than a year and were planning a future together. This had come about quite naturally, and we were very comfortable about the prospect.

As we entered the campus of Cartrefle College, the long, post-war, single-storey buildings used as dormitories came into view. To some people, these ageing military-style structures were an eyesore but I liked them. They were a little bedraggled and tatty but they had character. I certainly preferred them to the more modern multi-storey buildings that had been built between some of those old dormitories.

'Cartrefle', Welsh for 'home place', had been a teacher training establishment since 1945. Originally the college was part of a push to create more teachers after the war and particularly useful for training demobbed war personnel. Now, thirty years on, it was training a new generation of nursery, primary and secondary school teachers.

Jackie and I were in our final year of our three-year courses. As well as completing all our assignments and final teaching practices we were applying for our first teaching posts, so it was quite a daunting period. But we had few concerns so, overall, it was an exciting time.

We entered the lecture room together with forty or so other Cartrefle students and were greeted by Brian, who had worked for VSO in India for a two-year period.

The main aim of his talk was to gather a few new recruits, to tell us about the charity and, in particular, his own experience of living and working in India. As future teachers, we were ideal candidates for an array of posts in the developing world.

He told us about his experience of teaching agricultural techniques to Indian students. His presentation was full of rich anecdotes and colourful slides showing his work, living conditions and the trips he had made throughout the country.

It was a fascinating couple of hours, and possibly a choice for us in the future. For anybody who wanted to travel and broaden their mind – but more crucially wanted to do a worthwhile job in a developing country – it was definitely worth thinking about. But for now Jackie and I had more immediate concerns.

During the spring and summer months of 1975, we experienced a whirlwind of change. Our lives were morphing from that sheltered bubble of college life into the big wide world of work. First of all, we successfully completed our courses and were now teachers – providing we passed our probationary teaching year in our prospective schools.

We struck lucky and managed to secure those all-important first teaching posts. Sandwell Education Authority in the English Midlands was trawling the country for fresh recruits and we were offered positions in primary schools. Also, in a move to lure new teachers, they offered us a place to live. The authority was really trying hard to tempt young blood into their Black Country schools.

As soon as we finished college, we travelled to Pembrokeshire in south-west Wales where Jackie's family lived and were married. Within days, we had moved into a council maisonette in Cradley Heath in the Black Country. Joining us was Steve from Cartrefle College, who had found employment with the same authority.

As the three of us were already mates, we didn't mind sharing a home. We filled our maisonette with second-hand furniture gathered from friends, family and army-surplus stores. We met our next-door neighbours; June and Bob had five very young children and invited Jackie and me in for a cuppa. Weeks later, June confided that initially they had thought we were utter snobs because we didn't say a great deal. We were white faced and looked shocked – almost stunned!

It wasn't that we were not forthcoming in our conversation; we simply had difficulty understanding their very broad Black Country accent! It was a rich sound, with many words we couldn't decipher. We were simply inept rather than aloof.

Luckily, after a short period of time, our ears became attuned, which was essential before we started our new jobs. As the weeks progressed, the four of us laughed a lot about that first meeting. Our neighbours realised we were a little odd but harmless enough.

Yet more good fortune came our way with an opportunity to earn some cash. I found work for a couple of weeks in a nearby metal foundry. During the period when the factory was closed while the workers went on their annual holiday, casual labour was brought in to clean the vast area where huge amounts of molten metal had been worked. The massive building was filled with twelve-months' worth of heavy industrial detritus. The work was filthy, and we spent each day amongst accumulated grime and solidified metal splats.

Even though I was wearing overalls, gloves and masks, Jackie insisted I immediately take a bath when I got home. At the end of two weeks, when I had completed the job, we went on honeymoon with my earnings.

We took to the road, hitchhiking our way around the Republic of Ireland for a couple of very soggy weeks. We camped, walked a great deal, had some fascinating lifts and met a number of friendly – and sometimes bizarre – characters. But, most of all, we were delighted to be in such superb Irish landscapes.

One day we erected our tent inside an abandoned farmhouse in the Gap of Dunloe after a period of intense rain. When morning arrived, we found a flock of sheep had had the same idea and were also squashed inside the building. Looking at the quantity of sheep deposits on the floor, this wasn't the first time.

We were picked up by three merry farmers who insisted on taking us to the legendary 'Irish Puck Fair Festival' in the village of Killorglin in Kerry. There we watched the ceremonial crowning of a live goat high up on a tiny, scaffolded stage. It stayed there for hours while those below made merry. Quite bizarre!

While camping in Killorglin, Jackie unzipped our tent and reported,

'Some bloke has just stripped off in front of our tent and is swimming naked across the lake.'

We never did see the man again and his clothes were still in a heap two days later.

We also had nights out in Killarney at the invitation of a local head gardener, where Jackie ballroom danced with our male host. At a different location, we were given the keys to a show cave whilst the owner was away at Mass one Sunday and told to explore the underground caverns on our own. It was a brilliant two weeks in an equally brilliant land!

Returning to the Black Country, it was time to continue familiarising ourselves with our new environment. Cradley Heath, Blackheath and Rowley Regis were within this huge, urbanised region where our home and schools were situated. Not possessing a car, we walked and took buses to learn the lie of the land.

The term 'Black Country' is said to have originated from the industrial soot that was produced during the mid-1800s. The region was a place of heavy industry, with coal mines, iron foundries, glass factories, brick works and steel mills. Jobs were hard and families struggled continually to survive; poverty and health problems were never too far away.

More than a century later, such activities had declined. As in similar industrial areas across the nation, they were being replaced by new, lighter employment. For Jackie and me, who felt more at ease in natural, wild-country settings, this sprawling urbanised landscape took time to come to terms with.

My new school was a half-hour walk from home and Jackie's was a further fifteen minutes away. I was given a class of eight-to-nine-year-old children at Blackheath Junior School. A teacher from the year above was to be my mentor and help me in any way possible through my first year of teaching.

These were the days before the National Curriculum took hold, and what to teach the children was a matter of debate and teacher preference. There were textbooks to follow where mathematical processes could be learned and practised, but English teaching wasn't so clear cut. The children worked their way through a reading scheme then much of the language work, such as writing, could be covered in 'topic' work. In other areas of learning, the system was even less prescriptive.

As I had been to college in Wales, loved walking in Snowdonia and was married to a Welsh girl, my mentor suggested,

'Why not do a topic on Wales? It could involve geography, art, a little history and other areas. It would make a great display!'

I found the prospect of talking endlessly about Wales quite appealing. With rudimentary plans made for my first class and with the school holidays about to end, it was time to get to grips with the teaching. Down to work!

In the autumn of 1975, Jackie, Steve and I started our teaching careers. Jackie was given a vertically aged class ranging from five to seven years of age, with an emphasis on elementary skills. She took to teaching quite naturally and with few problems. Indeed, over the next few months all three of us had 'become' teachers: planning lessons, teaching, marking work and reflecting on our lessons. We organised our different groups, dealt with discipline problems, put up displays and handled a host of other incidentals that popped up on any given day.

We were learning the craft of teaching as it was during the mid-1970s. Having three probationary teachers living under one roof had certain advantages because we could bounce ideas around and help each other if we were experiencing any difficulties. But we all came to realise what a time-consuming job it was.

In order to have a break from school, Jackie and I decided to go camping during one weekend. Living in the Black Country provided few opportunities to get out into the countryside or, more particularly, the mountains of upland Britain. Mountain walking, caving and camping had been our favourite activities during our Cartrefle years and we were missing them.

One Friday evening, we made our way to a slip-road on the M6 and started to hitchhike, intent on travelling to Snowdonia. The journey took much longer than we had anticipated and we didn't arrive until the early hours of the following day. Once there, we pitched our tent for a few hours' sleep, managed a small walk, had another sleep and then hitched home.

We attempted this on a couple of weekends with the same result: it was almost impossible to travel to the uplands, have a decent walk, hitchhike back and then prepare lessons for the coming week. If we wanted to enjoy mountain trips, they would have to wait until the school holidays when we would have more time.

Our teaching was going fairly well and we were enjoying our work, keeping up with our lesson preparation, marking and the challenges each new day brought. You could never describe teaching youngsters as mundane! We both had some great children in our classes and, alongside the serious work, we were able to have some fun with the kids.

I've always found time for a joke or two whilst teaching – humour is so important for both the teacher and their pupils. One such example was when one child tied my shoe laces together while I was sitting behind my desk on April Fool's Day. Of course, when I tried to walk across the classroom I fell over, much to the amusement of one and all! (Mind you, I had already played several tricks on the children prior to that event.)

Most importantly, from conversations with our mentors, we knew that we were on track to pass our probationary years and become fully qualified teachers.

One day, Jackie said,

'You know, we should maybe be thinking about doing VSO. You remember, we went to a meeting about teaching in India when we were in college.'

'You mean work abroad and do what that bloke did?' I queried.

'Yeah! It looked really interesting. It would be a chance to see the world and do something worthwhile.'

The seed had been sown some time ago and we had agreed that one day we might consider VSO, but with all that had happened since finishing college we really hadn't given it any more thought. If we were going to disappear on a faraway foreign teaching adventure, now might be the best time. It made sense to do it before we became too settled in our careers and all the other aspects of our everyday lives.

We made tentative enquiries about working for VSO. Information duly arrived in the post about working for the organisation and the philosophy behind it. We learned about the kinds of projects they were involved in, which included teaching in schools. We looked at the pictures of some of the locations in which volunteers had been posted and several were of children in classrooms.

It didn't take us long to become transfixed by the concept. Surely this was what we ought to be doing? It all looked so exciting. The thought of travelling to a faraway destination in the developing world seemed very attractive.

Included with information were some all-important application forms. Realistically, we thought our chances of finding posts were very slim – we didn't believe the process would be easy. Even so, we filled in the forms and applied as a married couple for teaching posts. There might be somewhere in the world that wanted a couple of teachers in their school, so why not a pair who were married?

All of the questions were straightforward, apart from one which asked: *If you had a choice, exactly where in the world would you like to work for Voluntary Service Overseas?*

That caused some debate. Jackie announced that she fancied a tropical paradise island somewhere with sand, sunshine and exotic trees. I frowned. As an out-and-out mountain man, I would prefer to live in the high mountains – the Himalaya or the Andes.

Despite long discussions, we couldn't agree so we decided to leave that question blank. What would be, would be! In all honesty, wherever we were sent would have been okay with us. First and foremost, we were keen to work for VSO in a developing nation; we had a simple but growing desire to experience an unusual working adventure, to do something worthwhile and idealistic.

And, that was it. We both applied for VSO and we posted the forms.

Would we both be lured away to a far off land and work for VSO?

Were there some pupils out there somewhere requiring a couple of teachers to work in their school?

Chapter 2

Waiting

The story of how VSO came about is rather interesting. This international development charity was founded in 1958 by Alec and Mora Dickson. After attending university in the 1930s, Alec worked as a journalist in eastern Europe. When the Second World War broke out, he became involved in helping refugees in Czechoslovakia. His work must have upset the Gestapo because, at the height of the war, his name was on their list of most-wanted individuals.

When the war ended, Alec spent fifteen years working in Africa, the Middle East and South East Asia, training local youngsters to become community leaders as their countries gradually inched towards independence. As for Mora Robertson, as she was then called, she worked in Scotland in food canteens for the dispossessed during the war years. Also, during her younger days she became an established painter, writer and poet.

By 1951 Alec and Mora, both idealists wishing to create a better world, had met and married. In the aftermath of the Hungarian uprising in 1956, they travelled to the Austro-Hungarian frontier and, predictably, gave assistance to the refugees.

Alec and Mora made the perfect altruistic couple, committed to building a more equitable world. One idea they worked on was that young people in Britain should be able to help in the development of poorer nations. In their view, young people could be sent to these countries and provide assistance in a range of projects; it would help the recipients and be character and skill building for the volunteers. The Dicksons were convinced that by providing a year of service before going on to university, British youngsters could help create better societies.

The Dicksons' vision eventually gained traction in the British establishment. As a result, in 1958 the first sixteen volunteers were sent to work in Malaysia, Ghana, Nigeria and Zambia. Most of the first wave of volunteers over the next few years came from public schools, from upper-middle-class backgrounds – and they were all male. During their time abroad they provided unskilled assistance in the nations to which they were sent and in return were given accommodation and a small living allowance.

In time it became evident that it would be far better if volunteers worked for two years instead of just the one. In this way, their contribution would be more beneficial and they might gain more by working for an extended period. However, there were some who questioned the value of sending school-leaver volunteers; surely it would be more useful to provide professionally qualified people?

Consequently the way in which VSO operated underwent some changes. Eventually only fully-trained individuals in specific professions were recruited for a two-year period. Applications were accepted from a range of backgrounds, and women were encouraged to volunteer.

By the beginning of the 1970s most volunteers were teachers, but there were also doctors, nurses, physiotherapists, librarians, engineers and instructors in training colleges. By then, VSO was sending an increased number of volunteers to more nations across the developing world. Jackie and I hoped that if our applications were successful we would be joining them.

We continued teaching in our schools in the Black Country and didn't inform our friends, family or schools about applying for VSO. It wasn't worth telling anybody until we'd at least had an interview. This was a major decision; we didn't want anybody to become too excited, disappointed or outraged about our future plans.

Time was ticking by as we waited and waited to hear from VSO. Soon it would be too late to resign from our jobs if we were to start as volunteers at the beginning of the new academic year. Just as we started to fear that our applications had been rejected, we were both invited to an interview in Liverpool.

As it would take place on a school day, we informed our respective headteachers that we had applied for VSO and would need a day off school. Both heads were somewhat surprised but they wished us good luck. They added that we had both demonstrated our competence as teachers during the months we had been with them. If we were successful, the schools would be sorry to see us go. But there were a good few hurdles to negotiate before that happened!

Jackie and I caught a train to Liverpool, where we found the department on the University of Liverpool campus where we were to have our interview. We met a panel of three interviewers who wanted to see us both at the same time.

We were asked many questions: why did we want to do VSO? What were our teaching experiences? Where were we brought up? What was our own schooling like? What were our thoughts about the developing world? What were our hobbies and interests? Were we religious? Family planning and contraception? If we were sent off as a couple, there was a strong hint that they didn't expect three of us to return!

We answered the questions as best we could, taking it in turns to add any aspects of the reply that the other hadn't provided. After about an hour, the interview ended, and we were told that if we were successful VSO would contact us in due course.

Within a couple of weeks we had a phone call to say that we had been accepted. Amid wide smiles of joy, one of us popped the question: which country might we be going to?

From the other end of the phone line came the reply,

'Well, there is no guarantee but there is a vacancy for a married couple in a school in Jamaica. We will contact you as soon as we have more details. It's only a possibility at the moment, nothing definite. But for now, well done and congratulations to you both!'

The phone call ended.

'Jamaica! Jamaica! That would be just perfect!' I yelled and grabbed the atlas from the bookshelf.

'Look, Jackie, there are mountains! The highest are over 2000 metres! And there are caves! And beaches – many of them –for you!'

I was edging towards a frenzy of elation. Now we had a location on which to focus our excitement, and Jamaica sounded ideal for us both. What would the school be like – primary or secondary? Which part of Jamaica?

Coming back down to Earth, we knew we would simply have to wait. VSO would contact us when they had more information.

'At least we know we've been accepted, but we can't resign from our jobs until we know exactly where we'll be going. If we leave our posts and everything falls through, we could end up without jobs!' Jackie mused. Of course, she was right.

Weeks went by and we heard nothing more about our VSO placement; if we didn't hear soon, we would miss the education authority deadline for resigning and wouldn't be able to start our new jobs abroad. Once again, time was ticking and we were becoming a little fraught.

Then, one evening after school, the telephone rang.

'Can you get that, I'm busy at the moment!' Jackie shouted.

'Hello, may I speak to either Jackie or Roger Bunyan?'

'Roger Bunyan speaking.'

'My name is Michael from Voluntary Services Overseas. I'd like to talk to you about a placement we have secured for you and your wife.'

'Ah yes, we've been expecting a call from you. The last time we spoke, you mentioned a school in Jamaica.'

'Well, it's not Jamaica but it is on another island – one in the Gilbert Islands.'

'The Gilbert Islands!' I repeated. Where were they? I rapidly racked through what I considered to be a reasonably geographically up-to-date brain, but I didn't know where they were!

'*Yes, the Gilbert Islands. We'll send you the details of the school shortly, together with some other information.*

'*Fantastic!*' I announced gleefully.

'*Now, I need to know if you will accept the post so I can contact the school and tell them I've found two teachers. Would you and your wife like to accept these positions?*'

'*Of course we would. Yes, we accept!*'

After a few more pleasantries, the phone call ended and I stood in shock for a second or two.

Jackie called from upstairs,

'*Who was that on the phone?*'

'*It was somebody from VSO!*'

'*What did they want?*' she enquired.

'*Jackie, where are the Gilbert Islands?*' I asked.

I had accepted jobs for both of us in a location that was a complete mystery. Once again, I rushed for the atlas and scanned the islands in the Caribbean, assuming that was where they would be. The Gilbert Islands were nowhere to be seen.

I went to the index. Found them! In the Pacific Ocean! There they were, tiny little dots more or less where the Equator crossed the International Dateline, right in the middle of the biggest ocean on the planet.

Fortunately, Jackie wasn't annoyed that I'd accepted jobs on behalf of us both. To be honest, we were simply relieved; at last we could start the next episode of our lives.

The first thing we did was to inform our schools that we were resigning. By and large, our colleagues were very supportive; most thought it would be a great adventure and wished us well. There were a few, though, who didn't understand why we would want to travel to such a faraway place in what they imagined would be a challenging location to both live and teach.

More details about our new jobs arrived by post. We would be working in the Hiram Bingham High School located on the island of Beru in the southern Gilbert Islands. It was a co-educational boarding school for secondary-school pupils run by the Gilbert Islands Protestant Church.

All sixteen of the Gilbert Islands were low-lying atolls only a few metres above sea level. Politically the islands were in an early transition from being a British colony to becoming fully independent.

Among the information was an invitation to attend a VSO induction course in London, so off we went to find out more about our new jobs. We met a number of other recruits who were travelling to different countries, including a fellow Pacific Island volunteer called Nigel who was bound for Fiji.

We enjoyed a number of useful talks related to working and living in developing countries; after the induction, we felt much clearer about what would be involved.

Mirroring our arrival in the Black Country, our departure was another whirlwind of activity. We left our schools with the good wishes of children and staff members alike, then packed up our belongings, most of which we stored away in Pembrokeshire with Jackie's family.

Requiring sustenance during our final days in Sandwell, we paid a visit to our local fish-and-chip shop. As we walked through the door the proprietor recognised us.

'Hey, are you the two who are going off to teach in the South Pacific? You're in the paper, look!'

And there we were. A reporter from the local paper had been to see us while we were packing and asked us a few questions. There was a picture of us pointing to the Gilbert Islands in the atlas.

'Couple to join a sunshine school'
'A Sandwell couple are moving to work on a sunshine island, 2000 miles from Australia ... [they] will head out for the island paradise to take up posts at a local boarding school...'

The chippy handed us two carefully wrapped packages.

'Here, these are on the house. And good luck on your desert island!'

As we had anticipated we had varied reactions from friends and family, ranging from excitement that we were embarking on such a unique adventure to dismay that we were disappearing to the other side of the planet. We also had to endure a number of vaccinations into various parts of our anatomies.

During a visit to the dentist, Jackie's teeth were deemed to be fine. When it came to mine, the dentist suggested I should have my wisdom teeth extracted as a precaution, so at Birmingham Dental Hospital I endured a long and painful procedure to remove my awkwardly shaped wisdom teeth.

Eventually we closed the doors to our maisonette, picked up our large rucksacks and went down to South Wales to stay briefly with Jackie's family. While Jackie's dad, Leo, was driving us to Heathrow Airport, a car drove into the back of us in a traffic queue but fortunately it didn't delay us.

Once at the airport, we presented the necessary documentation and said our final goodbyes. Jackie and I were ready to depart upon our journey to the other side of the world. The waiting was over.

Couple to join a sunshine school

A SANDWELL couple are moving to work on a sunshine island, 2,000 miles from Australia.

In August, teachers Roger and Jacqueline Bunyan, pictured here, will head out for the island paradise to take up posts at a local boarding school.

Today Roger admitted: "It's an extremely isolated place but we are both looking forward to going.

The couple are quitting their Edgewood Close, Cradley Heath home, for Voluntary Service Oversees in the Gilbert Islands.

"We had never heard of the place when they told us we were going and we found very little has been written about the islands," said 23-year-old Roger, a teacher at Blackheath Junior School.

Roger and his 22-year-old wife, a teacher at Rowley Hall Infants School, will be teaching English and Geography to children in the 10 to 14 age range.

The couple married just a year ago and decided almost immediately they wanted to help the third world.

Roger added: "We should be there for about two years and I believe it will be good experience for us."

We were written about in the local newspaper:
'Couple to join a sunshine school'

Chapter 3

So, Exactly Where Were We Going?

We were heading for the sixteen-island archipelago of the Gilbert Islands in the Pacific Ocean, astride the Equator and, at the time of our journey in 1976, just west of the International Dateline.

They are part of the Micronesian Islands in the Pacific, which include Guam and the Marshall Islands. To the south west are the Melanesian Islands, which include Fiji, the Solomon Islands and Vanuatu, and to the east are the Polynesian Islands, which include Samoa, Tahiti, Tuvalu and Tonga.

The Pacific Ocean is one vast, vast area of water with just a few islands breaking its surface, and it was here that Jackie and I would live for a couple of years. With our limited experience of travel, flying to the other side of the world and living in an entirely different culture for an extended period of time was an extraordinary prospect.

The Gilbert Islands are geologically interesting because they are all atolls. Over many millions of years a number of underwater volcanic eruptions occurred in the region. Continual emissions caused the volcanoes to grow ever higher as the layers of lava built up, and eventually they emerged above the water as islands. Gradually the volcanic activity slowed down until it ceased altogether.

In the warm waters around these islands, coral began to grow and accumulate, eventually forming reefs. The final act of atoll making took place when the now-extinct volcanoes sank beneath sea level. The coral reefs that were left behind, continued to grow until what remained were sixteen circular low-lying coral islands surrounding shallow lagoons where the volcanoes had once stood. Having become a great fan of geology, it was a unique opportunity to familiarise myself with an actual atoll.

The islands have a tropical climate with a constant temperature range of between 26° and 32° Celsius. Terrestrial resources are very limited on the narrow strips of land that are just a few metres above sea level. Coconut trees grow in abundance, as do a variety of shrubs and other plants, but plant life struggles to survive in the poor and mineral-deficient soil.

Equally, due to limited food and fresh water, there are few native species of fauna living on the land. In complete contrast, there is an abundance of marine life thriving in the warm, nutrient-rich sea surrounding the atolls. It is home to an extraordinarily large number of marine creatures.

Even though these islands find it difficult to support life on land, humankind eventually arrived and made them their home. The earliest people to settle in the islands arrived several millennia ago and were from today's Solomon Islands and Vanuatu to the south west. These people, originally from southeast Asia, had perfected the skills necessary for travelling long distances in canoes.

As time passed, more people came and settled. These new waves were from Samoa, Tonga and Fiji and each time a different group stayed, they introduced aspects of their own culture and language. Over the centuries, through intermarriage and the mixing of traditions, the islanders' unique culture gradually evolved.

During this period, the dwellers on these Pacific islands called their land Tungaru. They survived primarily by living off the produce they caught at sea and from the coconuts and other plants on land. By digging wells, they were able to tap into the fresh water that lay beneath the atolls.

Disputes over land and resources flared up occasionally between islanders and sometimes resulted in battles. If the fighting became fierce, shark-tooth wooden spears and knives were brandished and those involved defended themselves by wearing armour made from coconut fibre.

It was in 1788 that Captain Gilbert in his British ship sailed in sight of the islands, eventually providing the European name of the 'Gilbert Islands'. During the 1840s, foreign whaling ships began stopping off at the islands and introduced a variety of goods to the local inhabitants including metal items such as knives, axes and cooking pots, together with beads and tobacco. Firearms were also made available to the islanders, with the result that internal fighting became even more deadly.

By the mid-1800s, a few foreign traders had settled permanently on the islands. Other ships started to visit in the 1860s with the aim of finding islanders to work on faraway colonial plantations. They were coerced or even kidnapped by so-called 'blackbirders' and taken to Australia, Samoa, Fiji, Tahiti, Hawaii or Central and South America. Some of these islanders eventually returned to the Gilbert Islands, but many did not. Also during the mid-1800s, both Catholic and Protestant missionaries arrived and became responsible – sometimes through harsh methods – for great social change throughout the islands.

A major development occurred in 1892 when a ship arrived on the Gilbertese island of Abemama. In charge of the vessel was a Captain Davis. He and his associates raised the British flag and proclaimed the islands a British Protectorate. This was at a time when a number of European nations, as well as the United States, were staking their claim to various sections of the Pacific region.

The Gilbert Islands, together with the Ellice Islands further to the south, became a protectorate of the British Crown, and in 1916 the islands became a full colony where Britain exercised complete control over the Gilbert and Ellice Islands. The colony included Ocean Island, also called Banaba, a raised coral island further to the west.

Colonisation had its advantages, one being that it brought about peace and stability and halted the internal feuds that were in the habit of flaring up. A system of government was set up throughout the colony, and medical and educational facilities were developed. Certain austere religious rules that had been introduced by missionaries were also changed to take account of islanders' traditions.

In time, colonial administrators came to the Gilbert Islands. The most famous of these British appointments was during the early 1900s when Sir Arthur Grimble worked as an administrator and later became the colony's commissioner. He was well known for his studies of the culture and traditions of the Gilbert Islanders, which culminated in his famous book *Pattern of Islands*, which has been read across the world.

During the Second World War, between 1941 and 1943, the Japanese invaded the northern Gilbert Islands. They remained there until the Americans overthrew them in the fiercely fought Battle of Tarawa.

The Gilbertese people continued with their subsistence way of life by catching fish from the sea and using coconuts, together with other locally grown items, from the land. Copra – dried coconut kernels from which oil can be extracted – became the islands' main export.

As time moved on, as in many other developing nations during that period, the islanders edged towards taking charge of their own destiny. In 1976, the Ellice Islands broke away from the colony to prepare for independence. The following year, the Gilbert Islands achieved internal self-rule in preparation for their own autonomy.

Our arrival in the Gilbert Islands during the summer of 1976 was at a time when the islanders were on the cusp of transitioning into a new, independent nation. Jackie and I were about to start our work as VSO teachers at Hiram Bingham High School on the southern Gilbertese island of Beru, and to be introduced to these unique Pacific Islands and their inhabitants.

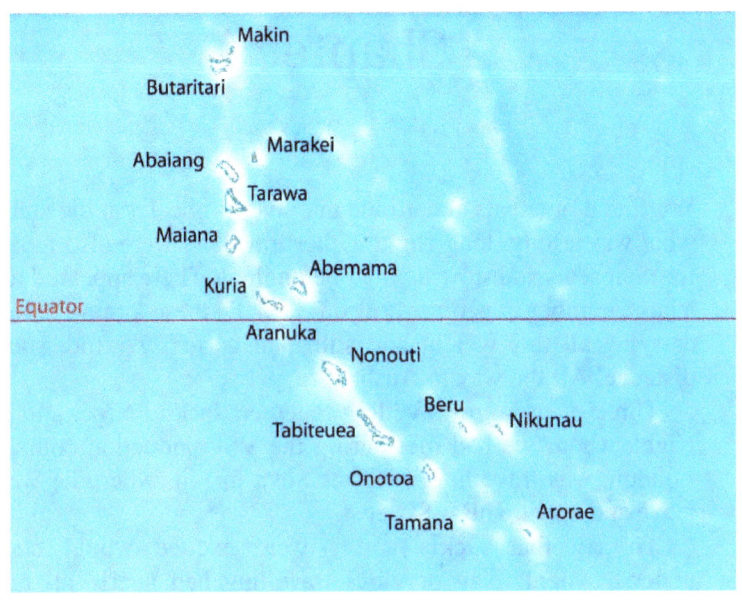

A map of the Gilbert Islands

Chapter 4

Arrival

We found our seats aboard the massive Jumbo Jet at the start of what was a long, long flight. Other travellers were also looking for their seats and stowing their belongings. There appeared to be a large number of people; how on earth did these aircraft take off carrying all this weight and still manage to fly? And, such a distance! All the way to Australia!

Three of us were travelling together: Jackie, Nigel and me. Nigel, whom we had met during the VSO induction course in London, was travelling as far as Suva in Fiji, where he would leave and take up his VSO post.

To say that Jackie and I were excited would be an understatement. Any previous travelling had nearly all taken place within the confines of Britain, the only exception being the year before when we had honeymooned in the Republic of Ireland. Jackie had made a few previous journeys with her family by car and ferry to visit her relatives in the Netherlands, and I had experienced continental travel when I had hitch-hiked alone around Europe for a number of weeks at the end of my first year in college. It was on that trip that I took my first-ever plane flight to Zurich in Switzerland on a cheap student ticket before I began hitching. Why did I fly? I simply wanted to travel in an aeroplane!

Jackie, on the other hand, had never set foot inside one before. What a way to experience your first flight! However, our excitement was mostly fuelled by the fact that we were journeying to the other side of the planet, as far away as possible from our own shores, to live for a couple of years in a different world. We were going to an isolated dot in the middle of the Pacific Ocean, a location most people had never heard of. Yes, we were at the beginning of an incredible adventure, and yes, we were very excited.

Once this massive beast was in the air, we settled down for the first leg of our flight to Bahrain. After that, it was yet more hours to Singapore – where a tyre burst as we touched down!

As the Jumbo doors opened so we could transfer into the airport, a wall of humidity hit us. We spent a few humid hours sweating in the transit lounge as the giant was made airworthy again. Jackie and I had just lived through one of the hottest summers on record in the UK in 1976, which we thought had been great preparation, but this sticky heat was on an entirely different level.

We flew through the night across Australia towards Sydney. Most of the passengers were slumbering, snoring, snoozing or struggling to get comfortable. Fortunately I had managed to sit by a window and, as we flew across the night sky, my nose was glued to the window. It was intensely black out there, with regular bright lines burning far, far below. These were bush fires; I later learned that they were a regular occurrence across the interior of Australia caused either by lightning strikes or deliberately by indigenous groups. The fires rejuvenated the land by burning off the natural detritus in the bush and adding useful nutrients to the land. Unfortunately, if they occurred anywhere near habitation they could be devastating.

Ever since we had taken off from London, I hadn't slept but had continually gazed outside. As a geography fanatic, I didn't want to miss a thing; we were flying halfway around the globe and it was a journey to be savoured.

At Sydney Airport, we waited a few hours for a flight to Suva – time to write a few postcards, which we left with a very pleasant airport worker to post. And then to Suva, our first taste of the Pacific.

We gradually lost height on our approach to the Fijian island of Viti Levu. After landing at Nandi Airport, we were met by VSO representatives and taken to a nearby hotel to wait for our next flight the following day.

With time to spare, Jackie and I enjoyed a short walk; after such a long time aboard planes and waiting inside airports, it was sheer joy to stretch our legs. And what a delight our stroll was.

Even though we were in a somewhat built-up setting, we sampled our first glimpses of Pacific island life. Exotic trees and plants lined the road, and there were views of an endless beach, a blue ocean and a field full of sugar cane. We didn't stay out for long as we were both feeling the heat as well as the lack of sleep.

The following day we took off in a much smaller plane destined for the Gilbert Islands. Halfway through our flight we made a brief stop at the small Funafuti Airport in what had been the Ellice Islands but had recently changed its name to Tuvalu.

Approaching Funafuti Island, we saw our first atoll. These islands were thin lines of land surrounded by sea; from the air Funafuti appeared as a green meandering streak with much of the atoll curve underwater. It seemed incredible that people could live successfully in such a place.

A few passengers left the aircraft and others joined. We took off again but soon we entered stormy skies – we were heading straight into a tropical storm! Below are my observations of the flight, which I wrote sometime afterwards.

The pilot's cabin was flung open once again as we hit another volatile bank of air during our flight from Funafuti to Tarawa in the Gilbert Islands. I was feeling distinctly nauseous as this small Air Pacific plane jolted violently through the wild conditions.

I glanced out of the window at the massive clouds, deep and active and all with aggressive colours, that stretched to all corners of a turbulent sky. I looked at Jackie, where she sat slumped and limply rocking from side to side to the rhythm of the storm and the ups and downs of the plane.

How on earth could she sleep in such turmoil? Suffering from fatigue due to our almost continual flight from London, we were both exhausted. Remarkably, she was able to sleep soundly!

Thankfully, we started dropping towards the airfield on Tarawa, the capital of this atoll island country. Last-minute gusts of wind tried to confuse and disrupt our progress before there was a decisive bump – at which point, land travel became the dominant force. We jolted along the uneven runway littered with coconut-tree debris. We had arrived in the Gilbert Islands!

As we taxied to a halt, the door was opened and a gush of hot, moist air flooded the plane. Somebody came onto the aircraft holding a canister and sprayed a repellent along the entire length of the craft, I assume to prevent any unwanted life entering the islands. That done, we filed off the plane and walked to officials who checked our passports and documentation.

Jackie and I were met by members of the Protestant Church who were keen to view their new VSO teachers. We jumped onto the back of a corroding pick-up truck with our baggage.

Somewhere in the past few months I had come across a list of a few useful Gilbertese phrases. I thought I would unleash my knowledge into this new world as I said goodbye to those who had carried our bags.

'*Ti - ack – aboo,*' I yelled with a smile. '*Ti - ack – aboo!*'

All I received back was a polite grin and strange looks. It didn't take many days to learn the correct word for goodbye, which is *tiabo,* is pronounced '*sabo*'. Our kind helpers were probably wondering what kind of an idiot was muttering such strange sounds on their island.

That is a lesson when learning a few phrases in any language: try to hear it spoken, as well as seeing it written down! This is especially true if there are only thirteen letters in the alphabet and many letters do not have the same sound. There is no 's' in the Gilbertese alphabet, with 'ti' taking over the job. '*Ti-ack-aboo*' indeed! How embarrassing!

We travelled along a deeply potholed sandy track, avoiding yet more fronds and coconut-husk debris. The vehicle came to a halt at the home of Kay and Tom where we were staying for a few days before catching a small island-hopping bush plane to Beru, our new outer-island home.

Kay and Tom were veteran missionaries, devout Christians and widely experienced in basic foreign living; they had worked in a number of countries for many years including China. They had lived through the most incredible changes whilst there, including the Cultural Revolution. Having experienced decades of living overseas, often in extremely testing circumstances, they were impressive personalities. One could only marvel at their bravery and dedication to their beliefs.

However, their job during the next few days was to brief us and judge our suitability for life in their school.

We ate a simple meal together consisting of items available on the atoll. In an exhausted, hot and confused state, Jackie and I tried our best to convince our hosts that we would be more than capable of carrying out our tasks at Hiram Bingham High School. Yes, we were young and somewhat inexperienced, but we were both willing to think and learn as well as being very determined.

We answered their questions about our teaching experience, religious background, families, interests, thoughts about the wider world, why we wanted to do VSO, and our plans for starting a family. We fumbled our way through these enquiries, but with the travelling, heat and lack of sleep, together with the general shock at being in such a different environment, it was all too much for us. It wasn't long before our hosts politely showed us to our bed.

We lay dripping with sweat under a mosquito net, too exhausted to sleep, somewhat bewildered, tearful and wondering if we had in fact done the right thing! Could we face the many challenges that no doubt lay ahead? Would we be able to cope in this hot environment? Nothing could have been further removed from our dreams of our new life than that moment. In just a few days we had journeyed from a state of euphoria to one of doubt and trepidation.

We lay together in the tropical heat under a thick cloud of unease and uncertainty but in time, due to our intense fatigue, we must have fallen asleep.

The following morning we awoke feeling more positive – the sleep had done us some good. After eating breakfast, Tom showed me how to extract water from an outside tank that stored rain from the roof of their simple bungalow-like dwelling. After priming the metal pump attached to the outside wall, it was just a matter of vigorously moving the handle back and forth to get the water. The liquid squirted out of a spout and into a container.

Tom suggested that I needed to get used to this chore as we had a similar contraption on the side of our home in Beru. One or two of the houses on the islands had manual water pumps that used water collected from roofs during periods of rain, but the vast majority of islanders took their water from wells.

In between the small useful household tasks Jackie and I were introduced to, there were more questions; bit by bit, they were building up a picture of us.

Later that day, we went to a gathering of some of the islanders, many of whom were attached to the church. Men, women, youths and children were all seated, waiting to meet the new foreign teachers who were heading for Beru.

Kay and Tom invited us to sit down in what appeared to be the place of honour at the front, and we were presented with refreshing drinks of *moimoto*, the liquid from inside fresh green coconuts. This juice from a freshly cut coconut from the top of a tree is one of the most refreshing drinks in a tropical climate.

A series of welcome speeches from elderly men followed, with translation provided by another member of the gathering. They all expressed warm and friendly thoughts, welcomed us to their islands and wished us success in our new jobs.

Then we were invited to say a few words. What? We were not expecting this! Neither of us was used to speaking to so many people; we were comfortable talking to a classroom of children but this – no! And, what's more, tradition expected me, as the man, to speak on behalf of us both.

I stood up nervously. With many eyes focussed on me in anticipation, I managed to say a few sentences about ourselves, how we were pleased to be in the Gilbert Islands and how much we were looking forward to starting teaching on Beru. I'm sure it was all a little rushed and incomprehensible, but the task was done. We just hoped that my speech had made some sense and fitted into acceptable conventions.

Eventually, after a few days on Tarawa, we flew 426 kilometres south-east in a small bush plane to the island of Beru, just south of the Equator. A week after leaving the UK, we were finally on the last leg of our journey.

As we flew down to the landing strip on Beru, we had a chance to take a good look at the island. The atoll was shaped like a fish-hook, around fourteen kilometres in length and barely half a kilometre wide. In the centre was Hiram Bingham High School, which filled most of the village of Rongorongo.

Around the island there was a reef that fell away abruptly into deep ocean. On the eastern side there was a sliver of land running the length of the atoll, which curled at the north and the south. That line was dominated by coconut trees that ran its length. The land appeared to be barely above sea level.

To the west lay a lagoon of very shallow water. The pilot expertly put the craft down onto a salt-pan runway and we bumped to a halt. We had finally arrived on Beru.

From the plane we caught our first glimpse of Beru

We flew over the village of Rongorongo and our new home at Hiram Bingham High School

Chapter 5

Settling In

There was much excitement as it became known that the new married foreign teachers had arrived to work at the Hiram Bingham High School. We were celebrities and, as is the island way, much fussing and feasting would take place in our honour.

We landed, were greeted, travelled on motorbikes to Rongorongo, were met by yet more people and then taken to the house where we would be living. We hadn't even started to unpack our few possessions before we were led into the school's communal meeting place, the *maneaba*. Each settlement in the Gilbert Islands has its own maneaba. For the school, it was also a focal point where ceremonies, feasts, traditional dancing and Saturday-night gatherings took place.

After our experience on Tarawa, this was our second time inside a maneaba. The building was big enough for the whole population of the school village to sit cross-legged around the outside, leaving the central part clear.

It was constructed using tree-trunk uprights, wooden cross-structures and a thatched roof that dropped to a person's height at the edge. The sides were left open, and there was traditional *pandanus*-leaf matting on the floor. The many pieces of wood and thatch were held together with wooden pegs and vast amounts of coconut string tied in precise ways that hadn't changed much over many centuries. It was a skilfully constructed traditional building with many ancient features, a beautifully assembled work of art.

We were led to the front of the seated throng; many, many eyes were upon us. Rikameta, our new headteacher, stood up and expressed words of welcome in English. On this occasion, both Jackie and I stood and gave simple speeches to say how pleased we were to be there. We told them a little about our past lives and how welcoming everybody had been.

Pastors from other villages across the island welcomed us. After more formal words and a series of prayers, food was brought in and placed in front of us. As guests of honour, we selected various kinds of fish, chicken, *babai*, breadfruit and rice. It was a feast. The pastors and older men, older women, younger women and finally children, took it in turn to take their food in that order.

It was a convivial setting as we all sat, ate and waved our arms to keep the flies at bay. This was an essential habit we needed to adopt as quickly as possible to stop the flies laying unwanted eggs.

We looked around at our hosts. There were men wearing open-necked shirts with either shorts or wrap-around *lavalavas* and women with simple *tibeta* tops and lavalavas, all of which were vividly decorated in a multitude of colours, patterns and pictures featuring island dancers and flowers. Everyone had beautifully bronzed skin, dark hair and noticeably healthy, toned physical features. It has been said that Pacific Islanders are some of the most visually striking people on the planet and the evidence was all around us.

In turn, they glanced at their new guests; it was strange and rather embarrassing to be the centre of so much attention; we were not used to the limelight.

The two VSOs whom we were taking over from at the school came to meet us. It was apparent as we ate and talked to Mary and Martin, who were also in their twenties and both single, that they had integrated well into island life. They had learned the local language and were obviously well-attuned to the nuances of Gilbertese culture. For a while, these two would help us to acclimatise. There were no school lessons taking place as it was holiday time and the children were with their families, many of them on different islands, so there would be time for us to ease gently into our new lives.

Before we returned to our unpacking, we were given a tour of Hiram Bingham High School. It was only a short stroll down to the lagoon side of this narrow island.

There were a few canoes next to a wooden hut on the shore, where the school's fisherman would begin his daily work. On a canoe with an outrigger and sail, he ventured into the lagoon to catch the fish for the day.

Moving inland, we came to the school's church with its tower still displaying war damage from a Japanese bomb during the Second World War.

We walked by pupils' dormitories, a large store and the assembly hall. Inside the dormitories were simple wooden beds where pupils placed their woven sleeping mats. There were a number of small homes for staff members and their families.

Next, we came to several classrooms, in the middle of which stood a large bell attached to the top of a wooden frame. The bell was struck at the change of lessons. The classrooms were made of wood with concrete floors and tin roofs. The outer walls were painted blue or yellow, and the windows had shutters but no glass.

As we peeped through an open window, we saw rows of wooden benches and tables with a chalk board at the front. The furniture looked rather old, and some of the dark-wood benches and tables had pupils' names roughly carved or painted on them.

On the ocean side of Rongorongo, we visited the school canteen where the students ate their meals. From there, it was only a few minutes' walk to our new home at the outer edge of school.

All over the campus were coconut trees, one or two large-leaved breadfruit trees and a scattering of jagged-leaved pandanas. Where nothing grew lay bare coral soil and scattered lumps of rock.

I was fascinated to see examples of honeycombed hexacoral lying around. I had last seen this in a ditch near Oxford, whilst completing a geology field study. It was evidence of continental drift; over millions of years, ancient coral limestone had drifted northward, ending up in the south of England. Some of these stones provided boundaries for pathways.

That was the layout of Hiram Bingham High School spread across the centre of this C-shaped island. At the narrowest part, just as we had seen from the plane, it was no more than a few hundred metres wide.

As the sun dipped below the horizon, we stood on the veranda of our new home. We watched the sky turn a vibrant red and silhouette the coconut palms, and listened to the soft swish of waves breaking on the sand. This new world seemed a little less daunting now. There was no sadness that night, just a realisation that it was time to start work in our new environment and our new life.

A few days after our arrival Rikameta, our headteacher, took me to one side in the maneaba after we had eaten. We sauntered over to the side of one of the main school buildings, where he opened a wooden door, and we stepped into a workshop full of woodwork tools and stacked timber. This place could have been anywhere in the world and it looked a little out of place in such a South Sea setting.

Rikameta asked a question which shocked me and completely stopped me in my tracks.

'Now, when do you want to start building our school fishing boat? All this has been left for you! Oh, and here are the plans!'

This short but stocky middle-aged man with his white shorts and colourful shirt, beamed with expectation and excitement. He explained that a missionary from the UK, gifted in woodcraft, had left some time before but had planned to build a new fishing boat for the school. It was a European design and was ready for construction.

I stood bemused. Rikameta had obviously been looking through my CV and noticed that during my school years I had taken a woodwork GCE. From this, he assumed that I had the necessary skills for such an undertaking. Brilliant. I was expected to build a seaworthy fishing boat to be used on the Pacific Ocean! That would be a huge contrast to my end-of-course coffee table that I'd made in school with a great deal of expert advice and assistance from our woodwork teacher.

I stood there, extra sweat dripping from my brow from sheer panic. I had assumed Jackie and I would be teaching English alongside a couple of other subjects. My mind reeled as I wondered if it was in any way feasible to even consider boat building, but I didn't want to disappoint Rikameta. This was our new job and we were working for VSO; we were there to serve and help our new school in this developing nation. But this?

Jackie had a similar shock when she was asked to teach needlework and other domestic topics – but no English. This was not what we had travelled from the other side of the globe for.

The next few days were spent tactfully convincing the head to reconsider our teaching areas. Fortunately, by the time the new school year began we both had timetables that combined teaching English with some Social Studies.

I knew Rikameta was disappointed at not having his new fishing boat, but hopefully this new arrangement would work out best for the pupils – and for Jackie and myself. I didn't wish to endure the spectacle of my headteacher disappearing in the Pacific Ocean in a sinking boat!

It was early morning a few days before the children were due to arrive from other islands and from villages across Beru. They were about to begin a new term and we were both eager to start teaching.

We searched the house for some food for breakfast; unfortunately, the arrangements for obtaining food were still being sorted out. Apart from the communal meal in the maneaba once a day we had no food, and this was a situation that needed to be resolved.

We walked around our large dwelling looking for something to eat but there was nothing. A classic image of a couple stranded on a desert island sprang to mind!

Jackie squealed,

'I've found this...and these.'

In one hand she held a long pole with fishing line attached at one end and in the other hand three fish hooks.

'You can catch some fish for breakfast.'

Why an earth did she assume I could do that? I had never fished for anything in my life! She was from a Welsh rural background – surely *she must* have been fishing at some point? She had frequented Young Farmers' meetings for a number of years; when all of those young farming types got together, what on earth had they been doing?

I pointed all this out to her but she was adamant.

'You can do it. How hard can it be? Look the tide's in, we don't even have to go out to the reef's edge. We can fish on the beach.'

Growing ever hungrier I decided to give it a go. The tide was high, the waves were lapping only fifteen metres from our veranda. I tied one of the fish hooks onto the end of the line and threw it towards the water – but it caught on some vegetation. Jackie unhooked it and I tried again, but it didn't go far enough.

There were many more attempts, including one where the hook caught in Jackie's long hair. *'Ouch!'* she screamed together with a few uncomplimentary expletives.

I continued casting the line, trying to catch something. After what seemed an age, to my great surprise I felt a tug on the line!

'Jackie, I've caught something!'

By this stage, she had nodded off in the early morning light to the hypnotic sound of the surf. I pulled backwards, the fish flew out of the water over my head and landed on Jackie's head. She quickly came to. We had caught breakfast!

'Now what do we do?' I enquired.

'I think you bite it between its eyes.'

'Don't you hit it?'

We debated what we should do. I looked at the fish writhing in the sand and had to put it out of its agony so I grabbed the knife and killed it.

After lighting a small fire, we cooked it. It wasn't much bigger than my hand but we both enjoyed a couple of mouthfuls for our breakfast. I was not convinced about my 'hunter-gatherer' abilities, but we did manage to eat something – even though we remained hungry.

Two girls from the village eventually came to our house during weekdays to help with the domestic chores. Fortunately, VSO had provided us both with an allowance to hire the services of a local person. Amina and Mitiera gave us a much-needed link to the subsistence character of island life. They found fish from relatives, purchased basic foodstuffs from the island store and did some cooking and cleaning, which allowed us to concentrate on school work.

Household tasks absorbed so much time in a place with no appliances, especially for those not used to island living. We had both enjoyed camping back in the UK but this was far more permanent; there was no option to drive off and have a back-up cafe meal or pack up and go home!

Our water came from our roof and was stored in two concrete water tanks at the sides of the house. As Tom on Tarawa had suggested, we had a bucket to retrieve water or we could use a manually primed metal pump; a vigorous back-and-forth action would sometimes result in water trickling from an old pipe.

We cooked on an open fire just outside the house using coconut husks for fuel. Over time we learnt to cook a variety of local foods, from fish to rice to breadfruit to sweet potato. Later on during our stay on Beru, I made a simple oven out of two cube-shaped Pacific cabin biscuit tins, each side around 60cms. With this, we made bread using juice called *karewe* extracted from coconut trees as yeast. We could even enjoy toast for breakfast, cooked on an open fire.

There was an old generator at the school that provided some lighting in the evenings when school activities took place but most of the time it was out of order. We grew used to hurricane lamps or, better still, pressure lamps (which required an internal pump to create a brighter light), both of which ran on kerosene. We adapted to all these changes, though it wasn't easy and made our domestic lives challenging. It was fortunate that we both loved camping!

Our house was situated on the ocean (eastern) side of Beru, the side with no lagoon. There was a little open land to the beach, then a short reef that quickly dipped away into the deep ocean.

The house was about 25m in length, open-plan and without any glass in the windows. It was cool inside, undoubtedly because of its large roof. It wasn't built of local materials like other island dwellings but made from imported building blocks, timber and roofing.

The house was of some historical importance. It had been constructed by the Reverend Alfred Sadd of the London Missionary Society before the outbreak of World War Two. When he was sent to Beru in 1933, he decided to construct a custom built house using materials from his family's timber merchant company back in Britain. Everything he needed for its construction was shipped out to the island, then he spent many months building his new home.

During his time as a missionary on the island, Alfred was involved in a range of projects at the school: house and boat building and repairs; wireless communications; dispensing medicines; Scouting; teaching; theological lecturing; translating, and even some surgery. This was at a time when Rongorongo ran a more comprehensive training institution in a mission compound. There was a printing press, several workshops, a dispensary, infant welfare centre and trading store. It was also a place of education for both boys and girls, as well as for older theological students. Alfred became a very popular member of the Rongorongo community, interested in everything around him and always active.

As the Japanese took over locations across the Pacific during the Second World War, it was suggested that all foreigners should leave the Gilbert Islands. Alfred Sadd refused to go. Not long afterwards he was captured by the Japanese and taken to their headquarters on Tarawa. At one point during his incarceration, the Union Flag was placed upon the floor and Alfred was repeatedly ordered to walk over it to demonstrate his subservience. Displaying huge bravery, he refused; instead, he folded the flag neatly, kissed it and handed it to the soldier in charge, which obviously enraged his captors.

One day an Australian warship came to Tarawa and sank several Japanese vessels, which caused further outrage. In retaliation, all twenty-one of the European and New Zealand prisoners were ordered to be executed. Alfred provided words of comfort and cheer to the others before they were all killed.

The Japanese chose him to be the first victim and he was beheaded by sword in front of the line of prisoners. Given strength by Alfred's words, as each person was killed the remaining prisoners applauded defiantly, much to the displeasure of their captors.

From the accounts of those who knew Alfred Sadd, his death was a huge loss; he was a much-loved man who always displayed great enthusiasm, happiness and kindness in all that he did. His house stood as a monument to those times and to his heroism, resistance and beliefs. Jackie and I felt quite honoured to be allowed to live in the house Alfred had built.

Later on during our stay, we asked why others didn't choose to live in such a well-constructed building. We were told that it was the traditional belief that, on the death of an islander, their spirits would travel northwards up the length of the Gilbert Islands on a journey to the 'other world'. The spirits always travelled on the ocean side of the islands, hence the reluctance of inhabitants to locate their homes on that side of the atoll lest they upset these important final voyages!

One of the recommendations in tropical locations is to sleep under a mosquito net. Thankfully mosquitoes on the Gilbert Islands during the 1970s did not carry deadly diseases, unlike in Tanzania in Africa where Jackie and I lived some years later where the mosquitoes carried malaria. When we were there, we had to take anti-malaria tablets. However, with Fern Amina, our toddler daughter with us, this was never a straightforward task. (Our daughter's second name was after Amina, our Beru house girl.)

Malaria wasn't an issue in the Gilbert Islands; the Gilbertese mosquitoes simply pierced the skin, leaving behind a small lump where the creature's proboscis had drawn blood in exchange for some of their saliva. Lumps occurred as a person reacted to the saliva.

One night, not long after we had arrived on Beru, Jackie and I went to our bed, a wooden-framed structure with a simple mattress resting on wooden slats. We made sure we tucked the bottom of our mosquito net securely under the mattress and checked there were none of the insects inside the net before we went to sleep.

The next morning when we woke up, my hand was completely swollen. We worked out that I must have slept with my hand resting against the mosquito net for quite a long time and it had been an open invitation for the mosquitoes to take their fill. My hand was so swollen that I had difficulty moving my fingers.

Luckily, Amina and Mitiera came to the rescue. They suggested finding the school cook, Rakaba, who lived at Rongorongo; she would know what to do.

Rakaba arrived carrying a container of a Gilbertese mixture that included coconut oil and a selection of different leaves. She rubbed my swollen hand vigorously for half an hour, then told me I would have two more of these massages over the next couple of days. For several of the island's ailments, it was traditional to mix a concoction of coconut oil and a variety of local ingredients for a series of three massages – always three. Within three days my hand was back to its normal size.

With Jackie and I reasonably settled into Hiram Bingham High School, and with our domestic arrangements in place, we were ready to start teaching.

Looking from the reef towards our house on Beru

*Our school bell - at the end of each lesson,
a student would climb up and ring the bell*

One of our school classrooms

The Reverend Alfred Sadd

The veranda of Alfred Sadd's house

Three of our friends at the school: Amina, Rakaba and Mitiera

Pupils at the school walking to their lessons

Chapter 6

Teaching at Hiram Bingham High School

So, who was Hiram Bingham? He was an American missionary who, together with his wife, Clara, and a Hawaiian pastor named Kanoa and his wife, went to the Gilbert Islands to convert islanders to the Protestant religion.

The missionary party landed on the Gilbertese island of Abiang in 1857 when a war-like feud was taking place between two of the island men, Ten Teiwaki and Ten Temaua. As soon as Ten Teiwaki set eyes on Clara Bingham, he vowed that when he had won the war he would take her for his bride.

By chance, the missionaries found themselves living with Ten Temaua. Fortunately for the Binghams, their host won the conflict during which Ten Teiwaki was killed.

Hiram Bingham made many attempts to convert the islanders to Christianity but found it almost impossible; he couldn't speak Gilbertese and the islanders were used to worshipping their own gods and spirits. By 1859, a church had been built on Abiang that could hold 300 people, though Hiram had to pay local inhabitants to build it because nobody would work for free. Even when the building had been completed and church services had begun, the islanders didn't take to the new religion.

Bingham, aided by Hawaiian pastors, travelled to other Gilbertese islands but the conversion to Christianity was a slow process. However, what he is perhaps best known for is providing the first written form of Gilbertese. He translated the Bible and wrote several hymn books and dictionaries. He was responsible for interpreting spoken Gilbertese into a written alphabet of only thirteen letters!

The part he played in converting many islanders to Christianity was eventually honoured by naming the school on Beru after him.

Time to start work. Rongorongo pupils began arriving from all across the Gilbert Islands; many had journeyed by small inter-island vessels that travelled between the islands. Some pupils were already on Beru, staying with relatives until it was time to begin school.

When the students arrived with their belongings, they settled into either a female or male dormitory. In total there were about 140 pupils from thirteen to seventeen years of age. There was always a degree of uncertainty about age, and some looked somewhat older or younger than their official age.

The girls and boys slotted loosely into four, age-streamed classes. On the islands, as soon they finished primary school a percentage of youngsters went on to secondary school. In the 1970s there were three of these in the Gilbert Islands: our Protestant school on Beru; a Catholic school on the island of Abiang, and a government school on Tarawa. To earn a place at one of these establishments, pupils had to pass an entrance exam.

A range of subjects was taught (in English) in the secondary schools. In our school, that range depended on which teachers were available for given subjects. When fewer teachers were in school, for whatever reason, the curriculum had to be adjusted.

For those pupils who succeeded in their secondary school education, there were opportunities to work in a variety of government jobs. Some pupils decided to return to their own islands and continue with a traditional subsistence lifestyle; others had an opportunity to complete tertiary studies in Fiji or even New Zealand.

Since Jackie and I had secured the job of teaching English throughout the school, we had to examine the available resources. We soon discovered that English teaching materials were limited to a few textbooks from the UK and Australia, much of which had a cultural and 'developed world' bias that we thought might create difficulties for pupils.

There were teaching materials from the University of the South Pacific based in Fiji, which were more appropriate to the Pacific island environment, but even so we spent a lot of time producing our own.

When developing oral, reading and writing skills, we relied heavily on blackboards and chalk. It is interesting just how few sophisticated resources are required in order to teach basic English. When needs must, and with a little creativity, you can make do.

Lessons tended to concentrate on discussion and oral work; we encouraged listening and speaking skills as much as we could, both in and out of the classroom. We asked students to communicate with us in English in the belief that it would be of the greatest help to them.

Some educationists advocate learning a new language by total immersion; in other words, it ought to be possible to learn English solely through the medium of English. However, others suggest that explaining certain aspects of a foreign language in the local tongue will result in faster learning. This is particularly useful for vocabulary; it is so much easier to translate the Gilbertese word for chicken (*te moa*) than to try and explain by simply using English!

We had no alternative to the pupils using English with us as we were not Gilbertese speakers. Neither Jackie nor I were linguists. I had a smattering of French and could just about order breakfast in a Calais café; Jackie was about the same level. However, she did know all the words to the Welsh songs *'Sasban Fach'* (Little Saucepan) and *'Hen Wlad Fy Nhadau'* (Land of My Fathers) – compulsory fare for most people in Wales!

We never did make much headway with Gilbertese and only picked up a handful of phrases during our two years. Jackie achieved more than I did. Was this due to us not being linguistically capable or because we didn't have the time to spend learning Gilbertese? Or, perhaps, both?

Jackie started teaching General Science but again this was somewhat problematic due to a lack of resources. Biology was one of the main topics and there were some textbooks to refer to, but many of her lessons started with biological aspects the pupils were familiar with, such as health education and hygiene.

She was also asked to teach domestic science and needlework. The first subject was challenging because whole-class cooking facilities were not available and the pupils knew more than she did about producing local meals. There were sewing machines but, alas, they were all in a state of disrepair – and not enough of them for a whole class. Even if there had been, there was little fabric that could be used with them. Despite the problems, Jackie did manage to teach some sewing to both girls and boys at the school.

The materials for teaching Social Studies were again provided by the University of the South Pacific: booklets to introduce students to aspects of life throughout the Pacific. These included text, photographs and maps describing island locations. However, these resources mostly referred to the 'high islands' (having elevation), which included Fiji, Samoa and Tonga, and rarely looked at atoll (low island) life. Concepts such as living in towns, using road vehicles, large shops, hills and rivers were irrelevant to a life in the 'one-dimensional world' of an atoll. (I describe it as such because most atolls consist of a line of habitable land with little elevation.) We spent a lot of time explaining the features of the high islands.

When there were references to locations further afield, such as Australia, the United States or Europe, yet more explanations were required. And what about life in the Himalaya or the Sahara or Antarctica? For a person living on a Pacific atoll, how do you begin to explain the life of an Inuit living in Greenland? That would be a challenge for most non-Inuit students, but at least for many there are books and other sources to help build up an image.

Most lessons, whatever the subject, were a constant extension of the atoll world together with an explanation of new vocabulary and its meaning. It was all about extending a view quite literally beyond the immediate horizon – not an easy task. With a lack of visual examples, it was asking a great deal of atoll pupils to understand the outside world.

This was made even more challenging by there being only one local radio station, Radio Tarawa. It provided a partial link to a life beyond the islands, but there was no TV or other 1970s' forms of communication. It cannot be over-emphasised how remote these islands were.

We were asked to organise activities including the Guides and Scouts. This was something of a challenge as Jackie had only briefly been a Scout, (yes, a Scout!) when she was brought up in Wales, and I hadn't been either a Guide or a Scout. This was another example of just 'doing our best'.

A central philosophy of VSO is the idea of 'having a go'. If a key element of the scouting movement is to develop a relationship with the natural world and become self-sufficient, then youngsters living in a subsistence island society were already experts who should have automatically received all those much sought after 'badges'.

Not long after arriving on Beru, there was a Scout trip for a couple of nights to the far north of the island. Martin, one of the VSOs we were replacing, was the leader. To be honest, he and I didn't have to do a thing during the entire weekend except walk to and from the location where we were staying. The Rongorongo Scouts made sure the maneaba we were in was comfortable - they really wanted to pamper the two foreigners. They organised the fishing, cooking and everything else. Such activities came naturally to them; they performed them instinctively and they thoroughly enjoyed every minute.

An important area Jackie became involved with was holding regular dispensary sessions for those with ailments in school. Within a couple of weeks of starting work, she was in action. It wasn't unusual to be woken early in the morning by pupils visiting our veranda requiring plasters or bandages for cuts and bruises. Here is an example of how it worked after we had woken up one morning.

'Good morning, Tentoa.'

'Good morning, Jackie.'

'Can I help you?'

The boy was swinging from one of the beams of the house; he had decided he liked the look of these wooden structures and he would have a little fun.

'Jackie, please can I have a plaster for my leg?' Tentoa displayed a huge gash on his leg, oozing blood and being attacked by flies.

Jackie carefully cleaned the wound, painted it with gentian-violet antiseptic and covered it with a large plaster.

As Tentoa left, a group of girls appeared on their way back from helping prepare breakfast for the school.

'Could you look at my arm, Jackie?'

Maria pointed to a nasty sore.

Jackie cleaned it before finding a suitable plaster.

Thankfully, none of these early-morning ailments were too serious and the pupils were fine with some antiseptic and a plaster or bandage.

On a few occasions, Jackie was given a fish or two after an adult from Rongorongo or another village had received treatment. Her precious medical supplies came from the Oxford Rotary Club in the UK and were organised by my mother, Florie. As soon as Mum knew we were going to the Pacific as VSOs, she had made a request for first-aid supplies. The Rotary Club had donated a range of them, which Florie had parcelled up and posted to us. Remarkably, they arrived quite quickly and intact.

So what was a typical day at Rongorongo like? It began with the pupils rising at dawn. The girls, led by the school cook, helped prepare breakfast, whilst the boys helped collect karawe, a nutritious juice produced by binding a coconut tree's spathe.

Both sexes helped out with the domestic chores then had a communal breakfast before assembly. This was a gathering in the hall at the start of each day, an opportunity to come together to hear notices, sing a hymn or two and say prayers.

At 8.15, the first of three forty-five-minute lessons began, after which at 10.30 there was a half-hour break. From 11.00 until 11.45, there were two more lessons.

At 12.30 there was a communal lunch followed by a rest period during the hottest part of the day until 3pm. This was siesta time for pupils and staff alike. Two more lessons followed before the pupils ate at 6.30. Between 7.15 and 8.30, time was set aside for either homework or extra-curricular clubs. All pupils were expected back in the dorms by 9pm.

As we were only a degree south of the Equator, the sun set around 6pm throughout the year. Sunlight drained from the sky very quickly, usually after a spectacular sunset.

Although the school had a generator, it rarely worked. If it was working, it was only available until pupils were back in their dormitories. For most of the time, Jackie and I used a hurricane lamp or pressure lamp, both of which ran on kerosene. The latter gave off a stronger light, which we used when we were marking books and preparing lessons.

When we were supervising homework, we often used our bicycles to transport ourselves and any exercise books. Yes, one of the perks of being a VSO was that we were given cycles. On more than one occasion we came off our bikes on our way home, even though it was only a matter of minutes! Cycling at night was fine if there was a full moon, but if not it was easy to hit a coconut, a rock, a frond from a tree or go down a large crab hole.

During a full moon, we often sat outside to read in the pristine air of the Pacific – as long as there were only a few mosquitoes around. We went to bed as soon as we were too tired to do any more school work.

Tucking our mosquito net securely around our bed was always necessary before we went to sleep. This was usually when we noticed one or two gecko lizards on the wall or ceiling. These slow-moving creatures have incredible pads on their feet that allow them to walk upside down. They were after mosquito snacks, which for us was particularly welcome at night. These green lizards have bulbous eyes, similar to those of the 1970s' UK comedian Marty Feldman. They were fascinating.

We also had resident rats! Not long after setting up home in Sadd's house, we noticed teeth marks on the soap.

'Amina, why are there teeth marks on the soap we leave out?' I asked.

'They are from the rats,' our house girl replied.

'Rats?'

'*Yes, rats. Rats live in your house. But they are good rats. You must leave soap out for them to eat. They like soap. Your house rats will fight bush rats and keep them out. The rats in your house are your friends,*' she explained carefully.

From then on we always left little pieces of soap around the house. When we heard scuttling in the ceiling, especially during the night, we knew it was probably coming from our house rats.

After a few weeks of teaching, we settled into a work routine and even found time to relax a little. One of the ways in which we enjoyed our free time was reading. There were a number of books around the school, and Jackie was particularly keen on reading on the veranda, especially when a pleasant breeze was blowing off the sea.

I'll always remember the day when she had her nose in a book and one of our 'house rats' lost its footing on the rafters and fell straight down onto her book! Needless to say there was a rather loud squeal – accompanied by a rapidly disappearing rat.

Over many nights, aided by a hurricane lamp, I read *The Hobbit* to Jackie under the mosquito net before we went to sleep. This was great fun because she insisted I create different voices for each of the characters. My favourite was voicing Gollum, of course.

With the constant sound of surf swishing up the beach, it's hardly surprising that Jackie was occasionally tempted into the water. As a lover of the sea and swimming, it was hard for her to ignore.

It was safe enough at high tide and on the reef, as long as you avoided stepping onto a highly venomous stonefish. These were to be avoided at all costs because their poisonous dorsal spines would pop up straight into your foot. The spines carried enough poison to kill you in less than an hour.

Apart from this obvious peril, Jackie could relax in the warm waters of the Pacific Ocean – and, what's more, it was right outside our house. On a couple of occasions she tempted me in but, as a person who isn't a great fan of water, my visits were extremely short.

My way of getting refreshed was to have a half-hour run. I had started running in the Black Country before we left the UK, encouraged by my brother, Nigel, who was a great believer in taking regular exercise. I had soon discovered the rush of endorphins that a run can release. During our stay in the Pacific I was determined to continue running, if for no other reason than to continue experiencing that feel-good factor.

One thing I didn't want to do was to run across Beru; I wanted to be as discreet as I possibly could be with my workout. I devised a figure-of-eight course that included running the length of our long veranda, along the beach, out into the rough terrain of the bush near our house and jumping a few strategically placed obstacles along the way. I ran circuits of this course for a given length of time. Once I had devised the course I completed it every other day whilst living on Beru and missed very few sessions. I am convinced it helped me keep both fit and sane.

We had started teaching our different subjects to a mixture of classes. Although there were many challenges in delivering our lessons, we managed to work around them. By and large, we thought we had made a reasonable start and even found a little free time. Working at Hiram Bingham High School on Beru was definitely turning out to be quite an experience.

A group of our pupils at Rongorongo

Jackie after having enjoyed a swim in the Pacific Ocean

Missionaries Hiram and Clara Bingham

Pupils working in class

The author running by our house at Rongorongo

Some of the younger pupils at Hiram Bingham High School

Chapter 7

Dancing and the Cutting of Karewe

Apart from living within an entirely new culture on the other side of the world, there were professional aspects to our new life that we had to take on board. One of these was getting used to working in a school where pupils remained on site throughout the week.

After finishing their breakfast every Saturday, almost all the pupils left the Rongorongo campus. From early morning until late afternoon, boarders walked to villages on the island and spent a day with relatives. Each pupil had a family – or perhaps several – on Beru where they could visit and feel at home.

These Saturday excursions provided a welcome break for both pupils and staff. Their extended families gained from having extra hands to help with their daily routines, and the visiting youngsters spent a few hours sampling family life. The young visitors took part in whatever was on the agenda for the day, be it a fishing expedition, a feast or simply enjoying life with relatives.

As the afternoon drew to a close, the pupils returned to Rongorongo quite happy and excited to get back to school because Saturday evening was the time for communal celebration in the school maneaba. This was nearly always a traditional event that included dancing and singing competitions and the occasional feast. It might take place in honour of a visitor or somebody departing. It was the highlight of the week and a grand way for students and staff to gel.

Traditional protocol was adhered to and it ended the school week on a positive and shared note. A typical Saturday evening comprised a competition organised by one of the four school 'houses'; staff also belonged to these houses and joined in.

Our head teacher, Rikameta, came into his own during these evenings: he was the enthusiastic master of ceremonies outlining procedures, commenting on each performance, giving lengthy speeches that held everybody's attention, saying prayers and providing the focal point for the whole night.

In every dancing competition, some of the girls wore grass skirts, colourful tibita tops and garlands in their hair. They performed limited movements with outstretched arms and bird-like gestures. In some dances, the boys came forward wearing lavalavas, shirts and garlands. Behind the dancers might be a crossed-legged group singing with great gusto and in four-part harmony. There was rhythmic clapping and a few men and boys banged a box to keep time and give momentum to the performance.

Even though any lyrics were lost on us *I-Matang* (white people – in other words Jackie and me), it was easy to be absorbed into the energetic and almost hypnotic mood. Indeed, it was quite common for certain individuals, mostly elderly, to suddenly spring to their feet.. They would then perform their own powerful and unexpected interpretation, usually after the singing had become louder and more charged. It was as though they were entranced and couldn't hold their emotions inside any longer.

Our school fisherman, Karikari, was a master at performing these impromptu, emotional dances. He exaggerated every movement and his muscles vibrated and twitched, his hands and arms reacting to the rhythm and euphoria of the moment. When all his energy had been used up, he collapsed exhausted, back into the group. This traditional dancing was always an absolute joy to witness.

Dancing is a major dimension in the celebration of Gilbertese culture. Similar performances were witnessed in 1889 by the American writer Fanny Stevenson when she visited the islands:

The leading man, in an impassioned ecstasy which possessed him from head to foot, seemed transfigured ... arms ... feathered fingers thrilling with an emotion that shook my nerves... All was poetry pure and simple.

Different dances are performed throughout the islands, many of which use feet, hands and body to imitate the movements of the frigate bird and golden plover. There are dances like *Te Bino*, where dancers sit with singers behind; *Te Ruoia* with standing dancers and singers behind, and *Kaimatoa*, a dance of strength where performers have their endurance tested by having their arms outstretched for a long time. All require great skill, technique, rhythm and hours of practice, together with essential traditional passion. It has been stated that Gilbertese dances are the most challenging to master in the entire Pacific region.

There was one dance, the stick dance or *Tirere* that was occasionally performed at the beginning of a school day. As we gathered in the school hall before lessons began, Rekameta might suddenly announce that we would all perform this dance before moving on to our lessons. The pupils and staff sat cross-legged on the floor and sticks were handed out, one for each hand. Even if you had never come across this dance, you would join in!

The idea was that two rows of people sat facing each other. With your stick you then had to hit other sticks around you – to the side, opposite and diagonally, five people in all. When the singing began, you became part of the rhythm and started hitting sticks in a particular order.

As you can well imagine, Jackie and I hadn't a clue, but the kind pupils around us were very patient and helped us out. As we fumbled our way through the performance, we received a good few hits on our legs, arms and hands, and unfortunately we gave out a few blows in return. But by the end of the dance we were hitting the correct stick in the correct sequence. After a few sessions, we learnt how to do it – and we enjoyed it! If nothing else, it produced a tremendous feeling of togetherness and was a superb way to start a school day.

We have an enduring memory of perfect Gilbertese four-part harmony accompanied by the click of three-hundred sticks. Priceless! Wouldn't it be great if such a 'whole-school' stick dance could be adopted in secondary schools worldwide?

One teacher at the school, Tametra, taught mathematics. He was large boned, well-built and had pointed fingers that bent tightly around his chalk stick as he gesticulated when explaining a point to the pupils. He was a jovial giant with a huge smile who laughed a great deal and had glittering mischievous eyes.

Tametra's classes were absorbing and his listeners hung on his every word; he was popular both inside and outside the classroom. At some point he decided that this recently arrived male VSO (in other words me) needed to be educated in island traditions. It would be good for me to learn a local skill, to become more familiar with his Gilbert Islands' world.

At some point Jackie must have told the story of my fishing attempt on the beach when we first arrived. This led to Tametra suggesting a fishing trip out in the lagoon. To harvest a whole array of marine creatures from the sea was essential for survival in these islands. There are numerous ways of catching fish and they vary from island to island, depending on each location's geography. It has been estimated that the Gilbert Islanders are one of the highest consumers of fish per capita in the world. Therefore, if an I-Matang wished to learn a local skill, he could do no better than to learn how to fish.

One afternoon I nervously clambered onto a traditional outrigger canoe. Tametra leapt aboard and paddled us into the lagoon. Such vessels have been used for centuries for fishing and inter-island travel; they consist of a slender canoe with a stabilising outrigger and are powered by sail or paddle. They provided the means for the first people to arrive on these atolls from faraway locations. There are amazing accounts of how island adventurers navigated across the vast Pacific Ocean from pin-prick island to pin-prick island. They used the stars, together with an intimate knowledge of ocean currents, wave patterns, cloud formations, changes in sea colour and the wind.

These skills were still being taught in the 1970s by some older men on the islands. Navigation was traditionally taught by looking at the maneaba roof where certain rafters and cross-beams represent changes in the night sky to learn the names of 178 stars, constellations and nebulae. The maneaba roof was considered an ideal prop for teaching navigation before journeys of any length were attempted.

In addition, navigational stones found on certain beaches around the islands were used. We had a navigation stone situated to the south-east along the beach from our house. It was a slab of rock representing a canoe set amongst other rocks and used to teach aspects of ocean navigation. We went to look at the stone on one of the first explorations we ever made, walking upon extremely sharp coral rock and in the glaring midday sunlight.

Our particular canoe didn't get far into the lagoon due to the inadequate assistance of its new crew member; the foreigner ruined the delicate handling of the craft on the open water! I had no idea what to do and found it difficult to follow instructions. Tametra spent a lot of time in the water trying to put right the situation amidst much laughter from both of us. It was a disaster!

After some reflection, Tametra decided that canoe fishing was too much of a challenge for such a beginner and suggested we go night fishing on the beach on the ocean side of the island.

'We will go at high tide and use pressure lamps and nets. You will soon get the hang of it,' he explained in his most encouraging and convincing teaching voice.

It was high tide, with gentle waves lapping upon the beach. We lit the silver lamps and pumped up the pressure to create a bright light. Tametra produced two nets and two baskets.

'Now, you must hold the lamp out like this, so the fish become dazzled by the light. With your basket on your back, you can then scoop the fish out of the water and flick them behind you so they land inside the basket,' he smiled. *'I'll show you.'*

He demonstrated. And, yes, in just a couple of minutes he had a number of small fish wriggling in the basket upon his back.

'Now you try!'

Oh dear! I found it tricky to hold the lamp and look for fish – I couldn't really see any fish because *I* was being dazzled. By chance, I managed to catch a fish in my net but as I threw it backwards it missed the basket and landed back into the water with a plop.

I tried hard to capture a fish, just one, so as not to look too much of an imbecile. However, as I poked the water with the net as though it were some kind of weapon, there was a loud crack. I had broken it! Another failure.

A few days later, we were sitting in the small school staffroom enjoying a mid-morning cup of tea and eating cake. It was break time and the first lessons had just ended . By mid-morning tea was very welcome after sweating through numerous explanations and generally concentrating during a lesson. As Jackie often complained,

> '*I start my lesson quite fresh, but by break time I've sweated so much my clothes are soaked and I could do with a shower!*'

Tametra had obviously been reflecting upon our fishing trips. Being the determined fellow he was, our conversation moved to cutting karewe, or 'toddy' as some foreigners call it. Fishing wasn't quite my thing but perhaps climbing up a coconut tree would be.

The idea of getting some elevation, even if only a few metres, in this sea-level land did have a certain appeal. It was obvious that Tametra was determined to get this I-Matang doing something traditional.

I agreed to give it a try. I've never been a great water lover so climbing up and down a tree sounded much better. Later that day we strode across the school grounds a little way into the bush and stood beneath a fairly small coconut tree. The various trees in each village belonged to different villagers purely for the cutting of karewe. Other trees were kept for producing copra – drying coconut flesh and selling it to make cooking oil.

The existence of karewe was possibly why humans had been able to inhabit these atolls in the first place because it provided a nutritious drink rich in vitamins. As Michael Walsh writes in his book, *A History of Kiribati*, karewe is rich in vitamin C:

> ...*virtually the only source of this vitamin in the traditional diet ... necessary ... for permanent healthy settlement in the Gilbert Islands.*

Tametra climbed a short way up the trunk using hacked-out steps and showed me the spathe with the young coconuts inside still hidden in their protective sheaths. He demonstrated how to tightly bind the spathe with string to stop new coconuts developing. He tightly bound it and pulled it hard to force the karawe to the end.

When he was almost at the end of the spathe, he stopped and sliced off the last part. Droplets of liquid started to fall from the sliced end and he placed a container beneath them in order to catch the karewe. Tametra explained that regularly slicing the end of the spathe allowed the karewe to carry on dripping. This was done twice every day.

Once again his demonstration looked straightforward. Being a conscientious pupil, during the next week I climbed the tree and followed Tametra's instructions to the letter. However, when I went to re-slice my spathe at dawn and at dusk each day, very little karewe had been deposited in my bottle.

Tametra concluded that perhaps this wasn't such a good tree; he told me that he had never used it much. Or was he just being kind? But once again he had another idea! He was such a persevering individual and on a mission to get me to master something!

'I know – you can use my best tree outside my house!' he announced with his usual large and positive grin.

'This is a good tree.' (He was too kind to add the sentence: *'Even you can't fail to extract karewe from it!'*)

'But, Tametra, I can't take your best tree. I'll probably ruin it! Maybe cutting karewe isn't for me. Perhaps I don't have the right magic!' My turn to smile.

No debate: I took over his tree. Whether he kept a very careful eye on it or I was blessed with a little island magic, lo and behold I began to collect karewe, a small amount at first that kept on increasing!

Early each morning and again before the sun would set, I climbed the tree, checked the spathe and was surprised at the amounts. As time wore on, I even went up during the day between lessons to tighten some string, re-slice or just generally look around and gently sway in any breeze. Hanging out in my karewe tree was very satisfying and therapeutic. Simply balancing there, moving with the tree, was indeed magical!

If I gazed south, I sometimes muttered, *'More than 5,000kms in that direction are the Southern Alps. Mountains, snow and glaciers!'*

A moment of fantasy, imagining being in faraway mountains, probably brought on by being slightly above sea level. Strange, you might think – but once a mountain man...

Whilst I struggled to learn to collect karewe, a number of thoughts came to mind. This traditional island society appeared to be far more in tune with nature than more urban or so-called 'advanced' societies. For example, the Gilbertese subsistence way of life was more conscious of lunar cycles; being entirely at sea level, it was obviously dominated by the ebb and flow of the tides. This governed the type and number of fish available, what kind of fishing was possible and in which locations.

Surprisingly, the spathes of coconut trees that were so important for karewe and copra production also kept to a twenty-eight-day cycle. With such knowledge, a person would know when to expect a new spathe and could prepare it for collecting karewe.

To recognise the stage of the moon at any given time was essential for survival on a potentially inhospitable atoll. Is such a relationship with nature something that 'more developed' societies have failed to retain? In our apparent sophistication, have we drifted away from nature's rhythms? It is amazing the thoughts that waft through your mind as you gently sway up in a coconut tree

After some weeks, I had two spathes flowing and I needed bigger containers to hang in my tree. As I returned to my house and passed the school maneaba, where Rikameta occasionally sat talking with elders from across Beru, his pride in having his I-Matang cut so much karewe was palpable. His proud grin was accompanied by amazed nods from his guests.

I also felt great pride in finding some success in this unique skill. I was totally chuffed with myself – and it was all down to Tametra's perseverance!

Some of the Rongorongo girls performing a dance

The boys taking their turn to dance

During some gatherings, everybody at Rongorongo, both pupils and adults, would take part in the singing and dancing

A local fishing boat out at sea

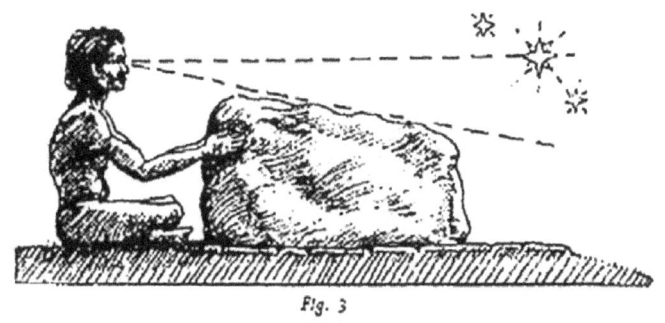

Fig. 3

*An illustration of how navigation stones are used
Courtesy of Gota, Ohnishi and Ishimura*

Cutting karewe in my coconut tree

Dancing in the maneaba at Rongorongo

The navigation stone near our house on Beru

The Beru navigation stone set amongst coconut trees

Chapter 8

A Dead Whale and an Inter-island Ship

One Sunday after morning church, and having eaten together in the maneaba, we were relaxing in the midday heat. Some people were snoozing, others were chatting. Unfortunately, some village children just outside the maneaba were disturbing this tranquillity. It was an annoyance for those inside because it was supposed to be the Sabbath, it was hot and it was time for siesta! But the commotion continued.

'*Te kua! Te kua!*' came an excited cry from the children.

There was some questioning and murmuring from the adults in the maneaba. Jackie and I didn't understand what the concern was.

'A whale has been washed up on the beach. It's just outside your house!' somebody explained.

En masse, we moved to the ocean side of the island to investigate. All dressed in their best Sunday white dresses, lavalavas and shorts, women and men moved to the east of Rongorongo. There it was: a dead whale upon the beach practically outside our house!

Apparently it was a young female whale almost three metres high and eight metres in length. It had a silvery-grey, hard, leathery skin with white blubber beneath, and there were visible bite marks around its tail and sides. There was general agreement that the deep chunks from the flesh were the result of an attack that had probably resulted in the creature's death. The whale had been dead for a number of days and washed up where it lay.

At one time the Pacific Ocean had vast numbers of whale species living in its waters. However, since whaling ships started visiting the area from the early 1800s, the numbers had been greatly reduced.

Michael Walsh points out in his book, *A History of Kiribati*:

Logbooks show that in the Pacific at least 30,000 sperm whales were killed: although the true number is probably much higher, because not all whalers kept accurate records, and because many whales were harpooned but escaped.

Obviously, from what we witnessed on our beach that day there were still whales out there in the Pacific Ocean. Peering at this magnificent young creature, Jackie and I wondered what had led to its demise.

We were not the first on the scene. A group of small boys were taking great delight in climbing onto the whale's back and sliding down the length of its shiny body, splat into the shallow water. For the kids, it was great fun on what would normally have been a mundane Sunday.

Like adults the world over, the grown-ups ordered them to stop playing. Even though it was the day of rest, it wasn't long before more people arrived ready for some serious work.

'What are they going to do?' I asked.

Whale blubber is highly prized in Gilbertese society; it is a delicacy. When dried and eaten by pregnant women, tradition has it that a wife will be less inclined to eat the flesh of her husband! It is an ancient safeguard against the cannibalistic inclinations of those who were pregnant. When a whale appears, many people store the dried meat for occasions when women might be expecting a baby. In a letter back home, Jackie described the scene:

People began to appear out of the bush with buckets, sacks and knives – the grand cut up was to begin. I have never seen anything quite so interesting – it was like striking gold.

During the following days, a continual flow of people from all over Beru appeared at the unfortunate whale's final resting place outside our house. Islanders hacked away as we watched the creature steadily reduced to bones. The work went on day and night; there was a lot of meat on a whale, even a youngster.

Iera, one of the teachers at Rongorongo, presented me with two whale teeth he had chopped out of the jaw.

'Here, have these. On some islands, if you have enough whale's teeth you can buy yourself a wife!' he proclaimed with a massive grin.

Eventually only the skeleton remained; we took several of its vertebrae indoors to use as stools.

After the hacking, the process of smoking the meat began so it could be stored away until required. The aroma of whale being smoked lay thick in the air across the island.

A few days after it appeared, I went off for my afternoon karawe cutting session. As I approached my tree, I noticed that Alaima, one of the school wives, was cooking some of the whale.

I climbed my tree and started tightening spathes, slicing the ends, retrieving my bottles and, of course, whistling while I worked. Males are traditionally obliged to make their presence known by singing in their trees whilst cutting karewe to alert any wives below that a man is close by (custom dictates that females don't cut karewe). I usually whistled Scottish folk songs.

As I climbed down, I was invited to taste this most prized of delicacies.

'That was really nice,' I said.

'Have some more.' Alaima offered me another piece.

I cycled back to our house with my karewe after consuming another couple of pieces. As tastes go it was okay but, I suppose, I wasn't a woman and I definitely wasn't pregnant! To be honest, as long as it kept husbands from being eaten, the taste wasn't an issue! At that moment, the entire population of Beru was very content with the unexpected gift that had appeared from the sea.

A few days later, Tametra, Jackie and I set off for Tarawa, the main island of the Gilberts. The plan was to board the *Te Maurie*, a small inter-island supply ship no more than 20m long. We were going to attend school-related meetings and collect some additional teaching materials.

Travelling by sea wouldn't have been our first choice of transportation because we had heard tales of extreme seasickness on such boats, but we thought we would give it a go. After all, we needed to try out all the experiences living on these islands had to offer.

We boarded the tiny ship at the very north of Beru. A number of islanders also came aboard carrying a variety of items ranging from food, small pigs, packages and woven pandanas sleeping mats. There was some amusement at sharing the vessel with a couple of I-Matangs.

'So far so good,' I suggested to Jackie.

'I don't like to say anything, but we are still tied up. We haven't got out of the lagoon yet,' she pointed out.

I was confident that we would have a relaxing journey across the ocean to Tarawa, a romantic sail across a tranquil sea.

It wasn't long before we entered open water. Then it began! We started to bob, lurch, twist and twirl as our meagre tub met the mighty Pacific Ocean. I looked at Jackie, who had turned very pale. We didn't need to talk; our eyes communicated our discomfort and intense nausea.

We had reserved a small cabin but we couldn't get to it. Instead we moved to the side of the ship where, if necessary, we could embarrass ourselves straight into the sea. And yes, it happened! It was impossible to hold back: we both vomited in unison into the ocean.

The ship was a mere toy being thrown around by a whirling water giant. This continued intermittently for hours until we reached a stage where our bodies could only retch a little reluctantly squeezed fluid.

Fortunately, by the morning the onslaught appeared to have finished for Jackie; she had ceased reeling and was sitting still but looked very drained. Faring much worse, I continued to cling to the metal rails of the ship and heave. And still the boat bobbed up and down, twisted and lurched. Oh dear!

'*Roger, the captain wants to know if you would like some food,*' Tametra yelled from the small bridge.

Not wishing to move during my discomfort, I glanced in his direction. He was standing perfectly at ease with the world with his characteristic jovial grin. He was next to the captain, who was evidently an old friend.

'*No thanks,*' I spluttered.

Tametra informed us of the delights the cook could concoct, all explained with a dusting of exaggeration and humour. In any other circumstance, the information might have been gratefully received but it resulted in more of that empty retching complete with the now-familiar sound effects.
Jackie remained still. I continued to heave.
Apparently, the *Te Maurie* had made good time, so the captain (encouraged by Tametra) decided to try some fishing along the oceanside coast of Maiana Island before we reached Tarawa. The fishing was productive but unfortunately the sea was very turbulent so close to the reef's edge.
At one stage between retching bouts, I remember noticing a lot of flying fish land on deck. They literally flew out of the water! I was briefly in awe before attempting to vomit again.
When we eventually arrived at Tarawa and tied up, I had been seasick for around forty-eight hours. Jackie and I were both feeling exceedingly weak. We disembarked and staggered behind Tametra with difficulty on a surface that wasn't continually whirling.

'*Good!*' announced Tametra, clapping his large hands together.

'*We will be just in time for breakfast in the maneaba!*'

Jackie and I plodded like the walking dead behind our lively friend who was eagerly striding towards a pick-up vehicle.

We both recovered quickly during the next few days and were able to eat and drink again. We went to a few meetings and managed to collect some textbooks for school.

We were invited to eat at the maneaba we had visited when we first arrived, together with a number of island dignitaries and several I-Matang. As well as consuming a fine assortment of food there were also the accompanying speeches.

When it was our turn to say a few words, we were prepared. We said a suitable 'thank you' and explained the teaching we had been involved with on Beru. Not only that, Jackie and I unleashed our secret gift: we had been practising for such an occasion and we sang a song!

We had been told that during such events it is customary to give something of oneself – a speech or a song. So, we sang as best we could the Scottish folksong *'Wild Mountain Thyme'*; that Gaelic-inspired song was perhaps the nearest we had to our own chosen 'mountain' culture. We did our best to harmonise – not as good as Gilbertese harmony but we gave it our best shot. We were very pleased with ourselves, and our small performance was much appreciated.

Fortunately for Jackie and me, we secured a flight back to Beru on the small inter-island plane at the end of our stay. As for Tametra, he decided to go back by ship. Oh, to be a Pacific islander!

One Sunday a young whale was washed up on the beach outside our house

So began, the cutting up of the whale meat so it could be smoked and stored

Islanders from across Beru came to collect some of the whale

Chapter 9

Large-Pawed Cats, a Prince, a Flying Pig and some Chickens

I returned from collecting karewe on my rusting bike. As I rode by the dormitories, I heard singing, loud chatter and laughter from pupils who were preparing to walk oceanside for breakfast.

My bike saddle had fallen apart, having finally succumbed to corrosion. Consequently I was using half a coconut husk to sit on! Unfortunately, this replacement never wanted to stay in place and regularly moved around, which made cycling an adventure in itself. Regular stops were often required to adjust my position. I was fortunate that my karewe tree was only a few minutes away – cycling any distance was a real challenge!

An interesting feature of living on Beru was that salt spray was continually in the air from the ever-breaking waves around the island. After a few months on our atoll, we noticed that there were many other victims of the salty atmosphere. Our clothes, our sandals and my spectacles all fell foul of it, each suffering degrees of degradation. Throughout the inside of our house was a veneer of salt: rub your finger over most indoor surfaces and you could feel it.

We eventually had to throw away some items of clothing; as for our sandals, we simply abandoned them and went barefoot. When we eventually left Beru, the soles of our feet were as hard as leather. Fortunately, my glasses held out except for a number of noticeable points of corrosion.

Returning home with karewe in hand, I went to where Jackie was making breakfast. She was sitting cross-legged beneath our lean-to kitchen outside our house. Holding a pan over a burning fire of dry coconut husks, she carefully cooked some eggs she had obtained. She had also toasted bread using a metal shelf I had fashioned into a toasting rack. Surprisingly, the contraption worked well.

As she sat lost in the process of making breakfast, smoke filtered through the thatch roof of the lean-to and created a blue haze above. We carried our eggs on toast to a soft sleeping mat nearby. As we attempted to eat, two kittens, *Nonouti* and *Tamana*, which we had somehow inherited, tried to steal our food. We had named them after two neighbouring islands.

Joining the happy kittens were a couple of baby pigs that were intent on running around underneath the mat! All we could see were two little humps moving around whilst we fought with the kittens that were trying to devour our food. It was animal mayhem and provided great entertainment.

Interestingly, Gilbertese cats were the result of a pure Darwinian natural process because they had mutated over the many years since their arrival. Cats, together with dogs, had most probably arrived long ago as stowaways aboard visiting sailing ships. They had either escaped or been introduced intentionally and were now found on all the Gilbertese islands.

Over many decades, all cats on Beru had developed large feet with sometimes as many as seven or eight toes on each paw. We often wondered how this could have happened. Had it occurred so they could catch rats more easily? A novel side of having such large feet was watching them walk with laboured strides. This was especially so with the kittens, who often fell over themselves because of their huge pads as they ran around and played.

So we now had a couple of kittens to look after. As an animal lover, Jackie was particularly pleased; she could have quite easily been a vet, worked in a zoo or, indeed, on a Welsh farm. Having such affection for animals was fortuitous because, around the same time as having two kittens enter our Pacific home, a dog was about to join them!

Amina, our house girl, was a bundle of fun. Happiness personified, she always had a smile and was constantly singing and on the look-out for some amusement. Both Amina and the more serious Mitiara were good to have around; they certainly made our domestic circumstances a lot easier.

One morning before class Amina, as bubbly as ever, appeared with a tiny puppy. It was so small that its eyes were closed and it couldn't walk.

'I have brought you a present! His name is Prince Charles. He will be good for you both. He will guard your house,' she announced.

At first we were not happy to receive such a gift but we didn't want to offend her. Amina explained that Prince Charles could be fed on coconut milk and mashed-up scraps of food. He would grow and protect the house, especially from the wild bush dogs. We reluctantly accepted her present, and so began the rearing of a dog we called *Charlie*.

Over the months, the puppy became a good companion and slotted easily into our daily routine. Charlie was an affectionate hound, always with one of us as we walked around school, rode our bikes or sat marking school work. If he stepped out of traditional boundaries, such as walking with us into the maneaba or church, he was quickly reminded by one of us or others that he had crossed the line.

Charlie was a quick learner. He followed us into our lessons, slept on the classroom floor or ate a fish he had stolen in front of the class while we tried to teach. This quite regular occurrence always provided much amusement for the pupils.

At one point, Charlie became attached to a decapitated turtle head he had taken from Karikari, the school fisherman. The dog took a real shine to this particular part of the hacked-up turtle, and he took his prized possession everywhere. He wandered into the classroom with it in his mouth, brought it into the house at night and lay on the veranda during the heat of the day just gazing at it. He was deeply in love with the rotting head which, sadly for the hound, was gradually disintegrating. Everybody knew when the head was around because Charlie's breath would be worse than usual and an obnoxious odour would prevail.

Eventually, after what seemed like a very long time, the turtle head simply disappeared. Charlie was in the habit of burying it safely in some sand each night; perhaps he had forgotten where he had left it, or perhaps it had decomposed in its festering state. To be honest we didn't much care because the foul odour had finally gone!

Charlie was particularly useful during school vacations when many wild bush dogs crept ever closer to the school. These dogs lived in packs in the bush, stealing whatever they could to survive. Chickens, pigs, rats and cats were all in danger of being caught and carried into the bush to be devoured. There were even stories of children being attacked.

The bush dogs, sensing the population of Rongorongo had greatly diminished during the vacations, were keen to exploit the school's vulnerability. These hungry hounds were tempted into school in order to scavenge.

Our missionary house, stuck on the ocean side away from the rest of the school, was particularly exposed. Wild dog howling would penetrate the night air as we attempted to sleep. After experiencing a couple of vacations where this was a problem, I decided it was time to act in an attempt to get a better night's sleep.

During the day, I placed a pile of stones along the length of the veranda then, as night fell and the bush dogs began their howling and creeping, Charlie and I were set for some action. At a particular juncture, when the howls were getting loud and close, we burst out from the bedroom and gave chase.

For a good few minutes there was a lot of barking, shouting and stone throwing. After a couple of nights of this, the three of us enjoyed better slumber – until the process had to be repeated.

So we now had three animals living with us. It was a good job they all liked coconut and food scraps!

We were waiting for the bush plane to land in the south of our island. Suddenly, we saw the landing lights of the craft coming out of the clear tropical sky and heard its whirr as it successfully touched down on the salt-flat strip. The usual small gathering had assembled to greet, say farewell and just stare at those who were coming and going on this twice-weekly service of the Air Tungaru trilander plane.

As the doors opened, we were greeted by John, our friend and pilot. We had first met John on Tarawa after our 'vomiting' trip on the *Te Maurie*, when we were treated to a delightful meal at his and his wife's house.

We discovered that Diana had been a VSO in Papua New Guinea and John had flown a bush plane to the remote village where she was teaching. The couple had become romantically involved and later married.

They had taken a shine to us out on our remote island. I suppose fellow VSOs have great empathy and camaraderie for each other.

'Hello, both! Here it is – sorry, it's in a bag, but I didn't want it escaping while I was in the air,' John explained in his soft New Zealand tones.

Our wriggling, white-bagged bundle was placed on a motorbike and we went back to school. At home we carefully untied the parcel to reveal a small pink pig! Jackie and I had been asked to rear an imported Fijian pig on our island as an experiment for the Department of Agriculture on Tarawa. The idea was to see if this temperate pig breed, originally bred in New Zealand, would flourish in the islands. Could it be reared as an alternative to the brown bush pigs found throughout the islands? There was a push to try and introduce a less fatty breed of pig into the Gilberts because the brown bush pigs were considered to be less healthy.

There was now some urgency to build a pig-pen. During the following days, as soon as we had finished our schoolwork, we worked on the construction. We used bits of wood for a frame and lashed them securely with coconut string. For the roof, we asked Mitiara and Amina to weave some thatch from coconut fronds. Eventually, after toiling through the heat of the day during one weekend, the structure was completed.

Tanraki, as we had named our female pig, was placed inside its new pen. It was essential that she had plenty of shade because her breed was not used to such powerful sunlight; we were warned to keep her out of the sun as much as possible as her pink skin would be prone to sunburn.

As the months went by and Tanraki grew, there were a number of occasions, especially when the roofing collapsed, when she suffered too much sun. We fed her on – what else? – coconut, karewe, fish bits and other scraps of food. Fortunately, she appeared content in her new home.

One morning, to my great surprise, as I went out to feed Tanraki I was greeted by not one but *two* lots of grunts coming from the pen! Overnight a local bush pig had decided it wanted some of the good life and had got inside.

My first thought was that perhaps it was a male pig after Tanraki but no, they were the same sex. We enquired around the village but this healthy-looking sow appeared to have no owner. We named our new arrival *Ezmeralda* and the two pigs lived quite happily together in the same enclosure – which we now decided to extend.

Around the same time, we were also asked to keep some chickens by the Department of Agriculture. We had to construct a pen for the birds to illustrate the advantages of keeping island hens in one place instead of them being completely free range. We made a pen for the chickens to live in by the side of our house.

John brought us some chickens, this time in a crate, on another scheduled flight. The idea was that keeping chickens penned in would make retrieving the eggs easier. The local method of allowing hens to wander freely anywhere and everywhere, resulted in many eggs being lost. It was also to stop chickens being eaten by bush dogs or taken by other islanders.

We became part of the Department of Agriculture's plan to push forward these changes and it resulted in us having a smallholding! The chicken run was also constructed of coconut wood and thatch, lashed together with coconut string. Luckily, the birds were quite secure and remained inside.

We provided them with a diet of coconut and a selection of plants that grew nearby. Every few days we gave them extra protein in the form of the insides of hermit crabs. We didn't have to wait long before we had a few eggs to eat.

After a few weeks of regular egg production, we noticed that there was a definite decline in their numbers. On investigation, we discovered that Charlie had managed to get inside the pen, pick up eggs and bury them in the sand outside! He didn't appear to eat them; he just liked to bury them intact in his very gentle manner. This compulsion had come to our notice before with his infatuation with his turtle head.

Unfortunately, Charlie sneaking into the chicken pen must have been witnessed by a wild bush dog. One morning, not long after catching our dog performing his egg-thieving trick, I caught a bush dog inside the pen! Sadly, it had killed one of our chickens.

After Charlie and I had chased it away, some serious reinforcement of the enclosure took place. For the remainder of our time on Beru, our chickens continued to produce eggs without more visits from any dogs.

There were occasions when Jackie and I wanted a chicken to eat but didn't want to take one of our 'government' birds. Similar to obtaining a fish, sometimes we could purchase a chicken from villagers (the currency of the Gilbert Islands was the Australian dollar). One day, Jackie asked Amina to do just that. Here is the tale of the 'homing' chicken taken from a letter Jackie wrote:

I gave Amina a dollar in order to buy a chicken in the village. She brought a chicken back, put it in the house and tied it to a chair. But it escaped and Amina chased it all the way back to the village. This happened twice, with the very same bird! I'm beginning to think this is some kind of trick – a homing chicken! Come to think of it, Amina is in the village looking for another chicken right now. Let's keep our fingers crossed this time.

We had encounters with other pigs on the island, perhaps because we'd taken in one bush pig to live with Tanraki, our Fijian pink pig. There was a period when other bush pigs were seen around our house. On one occasion, our island policeman arrived with two helpers to catch a couple of these rogue animals. I went to help them scour the bush and beach near to our house, but to no avail. Tiaki, the Beru constable, explained that pigs weren't supposed to roam freely and he was planning on catching the offending creatures. But, from what we had realised from our now very content Ezmeralda bush pig, there were plenty of unattached hogs still out there.

As our smallholding became established, we reported back on our progress to the Department of Agriculture. Our experience was noted and helped in setting up other pig and chicken runs on other islands. There was some interest in having pens on Beru, but the old way of letting the creatures run free prevailed.

Kristian, our school caretaker, said he would look after the livestock if we ever went off the island; he could see the benefit of keeping the pens. Eventually the experiment ended but Jackie and I had had a lot of fun with all these animals who really enriched our lives on our island.

Charlie

Jackie in our outside kitchen

Tanraki

Jackie sweeping around our kitchen

Chapter 10

Out and About

Everyday life on our island continued. In addition to working in school and caring for our animals, we occasionally had chance to get out and about on Beru.

A fairly regular trip was to cycle to a small store in Nuka, the island's main village, about a kilometre or so away. Periodically, depending on what the supply ship had dropped off, it was possible to pick up an array of interesting goodies. Over time we came across a variety of items in this small shack, some more out of place than others. These ranged from cans of Coke, Vegemite (a savoury Australian spread for toast, similar to Marmite), Brylcreem hair gel (popular during the 1950s), and pyjamas – all of which appeared only once. If you went back on another day, you would probably be disappointed as they were delights from a visiting ship for that one time only.

The selection of items deposited by the inter-island vessel were very random. However, one regular item that was in great demand across Beru was kerosene, mainly required for lighting hurricane and pressure lamps.

Jackie and I needed kerosene for more than that because there was a kerosene-powered refrigerator in Sadd's house . A fridge, no less! After having had some instruction whilst on Tarawa, I endeavoured to keep it working but I can honestly say that the refrigerator was the bane of our lives. It didn't matter how much I cleaned the various components and trimmed the wick, it never worked properly. Whether it decided to work or not was just sheer chance.

Batteries for radios were also in demand amongst the islanders. Many homes had a radio where people could tune into Radio Tarawa, a station that provided a mixture of Gilbert Island news and music, the latter including popular local singing and some overseas music.

While we were at the school, *'Happy Hawaii'* by Abba was a great favourite with the pupils. This number by the famous Swedish band was popular on Radio Tarawa. Whenever the children sang the song the harmonies were just as good as Abba's, if rather different.

Jackie and I were also on the look-out for batteries for our radio, but unfortunately the ones that occasionally turned up in the Nuka store didn't last very long – we suspected this was due to their age.

We were always keen to listen to news from the outside world on the radio we had brought with us from the UK. Depending on the atmospherics and air-wave interference at different times of the day, we could sometimes pick-up the *BBC World Service, Voice of America* or *Radio Moscow*. If the conditions allowed, the fun part was to listen to them and try to recognise any propaganda. The same items often had a completely different twist to them depending on who was reporting – after all, it was the height of the Cold War.

A particular delight on Sunday evenings was *Doctor Finlay's Casebook* on *Radio Fiji*. This drama programme, produced by the BBC and sold to the Fijians, was about fictitious medical cases encountered by a Scottish Highland doctor during the 1920s. Each episode was about a different event in Doctor Finlay's life.

We both became hooked on those Scottish accents; it was pure indulgence and reminded us of our previous lives. It was also far removed from our present situation on our Pacific atoll! However, tuning in to the weak Radio Fiji signal each Sunday was a massive problem. The sound was often poor and invariably accompanied by strange atmospheric noises, then sometimes the signal disappeared altogether.

Happily, we found a couple of solutions to our problem. One was to leave the batteries out all day before the broadcast so the heat of the strong equatorial sun gave them an extra boost before they were needed during the evening. The other thing that worked well was to attach a wire to the radio aerial, push it out from under our mosquito net (we always listened to the programme in bed, away from the biting insects), through the window, across open land and onto a thicker wire draped between two coconut trees.

The thicker wire had been left from Alfred Sadd's days; he had used it to send secret radio reports to Allied forces during the Japanese invasion. This substantial wire stretched some fifteen metres or so from one coconut trunk to another. Attaching our wire to it, together with those sun-infused batteries, often did the trick!

Travelling to Nuka was always interesting. Once in the village, I enjoyed looking around and taking in the scene. Nestled quite naturally amongst the thin coconut tree trunks, with their star-shaped fronds, were a cluster of homes. These were constructed from coconut and pandanus wood, raised off the ground and had open sides and thatched roofs.

Sometimes I would see a few people inside chatting, holding infants or reclining and resting. Outside, men, women and children might be going about their daily chores: carrying a catch of fish; walking with containers of karewe, husking coconuts; lighting a fire ready for cooking; raking leaves; cleaning fish or washing utensils.

I was always fascinated by how youngsters were regularly left in charge of cooking. I distinctly remember seeing a girl of around seven years of age with a young toddler on her hips, holding a bloodied knife and about to cook fish on an open fire. She accepted this responsibility quite naturally, only occasionally commenting to her young friends around her about the game they were playing.

It was a popular game where the children attached a long coconut frond to the end of a dragonfly's abdomen. They cut the frond very precisely so that it kept the insect hovering at the same height and it did not fly away.

Jackie and I admired the way children were given such responsibility and were more than capable of handling what some might consider to be potentially dangerous chores. Such domestic expectations were simply part of society.

These scenarios intrigued us. Could people in so-called 'developed' locations in the world possibly give more responsibility to their young children? Or had those youngsters become far too protected within their societies?

As I cycled along the dirt track through Nuka on the way to the village store, I sometimes caused a stir. There were shouts of I-Matang as I cycled; as a white European, I stood out like a sore thumb. People stared and sometimes pointed or chuckled as I trundled along.

I remember relating this to how anyone who is different in some way is sometimes acknowledged by locals; as a result, Jackie and I have always felt empathy for minority groups, especially if they are treated negatively and discriminated against. That most certainly wasn't the case for us on Beru; indeed, we were held in high regard as I-Matangs on the islands.

On one jaunt on her bike, Jackie ended up in a maneaba at Taboiaki in the south of our island. I was teaching, so she had gone off by herself. As a guest, Jackie was immediately thrust to the front of the packed maneaba. Unbeknown to her, it was a special occasion where a muddy-looking liquid mixed with grated coconut, known as *bokaboka*, was being taken and drunk from nearby ponds. It was an ancient custom where an algae had been specifically produced to survive during storms, or when there had been a drought and obtaining food might be a problem. This drink helped people endure the crisis until better times arrived. The bokaboka grew in large shallow ponds cleverly constructed from coral stone.

'Would the I-Matang like to go to the toilet?' was the message that made its way round to Jackie as she sat waiting to drink the bokaboka.

'No, I'm fine, thank you.'

Jackie was sent a number of other messages and questions that circled back and forth among the gathering before the drinking of the liquid began. She repeated that she felt fine and didn't require the toilet or anything else.

All eyes fell upon her and her hosts studied her reaction as the liquid flowed down her throat. She smiled and nodded with delight as the last drops past her lips.

'Here, have some more!' her hosts insisted.

'Thank you,' she replied.

The algae is unique to the islands and had, over the centuries, saved a good number of Beru islanders' lives. Bokaboka is evidence of the ingenuity of these island people. When required, humans can survive in the most hostile and challenging of circumstances; it is in our nature to survive.

The longer we lived on the island, the more our eyes were opened to its traditions. Like most other societies, there were many beliefs and ancient ways within the Gilbert Islands. From old legends explaining how the islands were first made, to stories referring to supernatural occurrences, to historical rituals required for particular activities, the islands had them all.

Quite how such ancient beliefs squared with religious requirements that had arrived in more recent times was another matter. These two quite different ways of living, which ought to have been in opposition, appeared to live alongside each other. Gilbertese people believed in many of the ancient ways but were also active members of a church.

Although Jackie and I didn't witness the following event, we certainly heard about it. There was one occasion when islanders met in Beru's main maneaba in Nuka. Human bones from ancestors had been lifted down from the rafters where they had been placed for decades. The bones were then washed in the lagoon and freshly oiled. This cleansing took place at a specific time on the calendar.

A couple of days after the ceremony, the lagoon filled with thousands of small fish, which were said to be a gift from the forebears in appreciation of their bones being cleaned. To rational and logical-thinking outsider, there had to be some reasonable explanation: was it the state of the tides or weather patterns? But, as far as we could ascertain, there appeared to be no scientific explanation.

The American explorer Charles Wilkes witnessed similar scenes during his journeys to these islands during the mid-1800s:

The skulls of their ancestors are carefully preserved by their family and held in great reverence ... these skulls are taken down, wreathed with leaves, laid on a new mat, anointed with oil, and presented with food.

We had been encouraged to read Arthur Grimble's *A Pattern of Islands* before embarking on our journey to the Pacific. It was an enlightening record of a British colonial officer's experiences in the Gilbert Islands in the 1900s. It detailed many traditional ways of island life, including numerous references to 'magic' spells and rituals. Grimble outlined a variety of spells including those for porpoise calling, killing a foe, stopping pilfering, becoming a good dancer and procuring a lover.

Certain rituals were carried out in everyday life for, say, building a new maneaba or a canoe. For us, as visitors to this traditional world, there were inexplicable occurrences that did not fit tidily into our modern, so-called sophisticated ways of thinking. Such incidents still baffle us to this day!

An interesting domestic feature visible whilst journeying along the lagoon side of the island were the toilets. In our house we had a toilet that went straight into a cesspit at the side of the house. This was the only one on our island, designed and built by the missionary Alfred Sadd. To flush it, we had a bucket of water that we needed to collect from one of our water tanks at the side of the building.

All other toileting on Beru took place on *nagataris*. Each village had a wooden plankway built out over the lagoon, at the end of which was a small, thatched structure. This was a toilet from which the waste dropped into the shallow sea below. Visiting the toilet involved walking out over the water on a plank and squatting over a hole inside a small, thatched shelter.

The ingenious part of this system was that, twice each day, the tide created a natural flush and took away the waste from beneath the nagatari. It was a win-win situation, which, in turn, provided extra food for fish and other creatures living in the lagoon. All nagataris throughout the Gilberts were constructed on the lagoon side of the islands.

We soon learnt that going to the toilet was more of a social affair than in other places around the world. A visit might be an occasion when a few people went off together for a gossip. Foreigners' hang-ups and prudishness over such matters was not entirely understood and provided a certain amount of amusement.

Jackie experienced numerous occasions when either Amina or Mitiara would sit cross-legged on the floor chatting whilst she went to the toilet in our house. Occasionally, as I sat on the toilet, I even had buckets of water thrown over me just for a little fun! This produced a lot of laughter (including Jackie's) as I tried to concentrate on the loo.

As I said, bikes were useful to get around locally. One day on her way back from the Nuka store, Jackie stopped off to have a cup of tea and a chat with a missionary sister from France.

Sister Mary lived in the only Catholic village on Beru, Bwariti (the Gilbertese spelling for Paris). The southern Gilbert Islands were predominantly Protestant and the northern islands were mainly Catholic due to the success each religious missionary group had been in converting the locals when they arrived.

The animosity between the two religious groups had been imported from Europe and was maintained even within this far-flung region. Needless to say, the villagers of Bwariti didn't always get together with those from the rest of the island and vice versa.

Whilst Jackie and the sister were chatting, the conversation eventually got around to her host's injured leg. Jackie examined the wound and decided that it needed medical attention; in her opinion, it looked like a serious infection as a blue line could be seen travelling up her leg.

It wasn't in Sister Mary's nature to make a big fuss about her own health and she said that her leg would soon improve with a little rest; such is the way of many who are devoted to their calling.

Jackie wasn't happy, however. She had been working in her capacity as dispenser at the school for some months and was continually on the look-out for ailments and infections. Alarm bells were ringing. It looked very much like blood poisoning and, if left, could result in serious illness or worse.

Sister Mary had met her match and, after a lot of insistence, Jackie persuaded her to fly to Tarawa. Luckily she secured a seat on the next plane to the main island where she was treated for blood poisoning. After a couple of weeks, Sister Mary was able to return to Beru. Never let it be said that the occasional chit-chat over a cuppa is a waste of time.

During the time we lived on the Gilbert Islands, 1976 to 1978, the group of islands was transitioning between being a British colony and a fully independent nation. As a British colony, it had become a tradition to celebrate Queen Elizabeth's birthday. For those of us at Hiram Bingham High School, this manifested itself with a school march along the island and then back again. On these occasions, the pupils donned their Scout and Guide uniforms and paraded across Beru. As Jackie and I were in charge of the school Guides and Scouts, we also took part.

The Girl Guides at the school, which included all the older girls, wore a blue dress and neckerchief. The Boy Scouts, again consisting of the older boys, wore either blue lavalavas and white shorts or white shorts, white shirt and neckerchief. As leader, Jackie had her blue Guide dress on and I wore a white shirt and shorts.

Jackie and I rode our bicycles at the rear of the parade – I found this useful whenever I wanted to zoom off and take photographs. Two students held Guide and Scout flags as they marched along.

As with so many aspects of school life, the students knew precisely where and how to march in an organised and controlled manner. The event took place over one morning. Once we reached a certain point after crossing the causeway at Nuka, we paraded in front of a flagpole before turning around and marching back.

On the face of it, the notion of celebrating the birthday of a queen of a faraway, wealthy and developed land on the other side of the planet seemed a tad surreal. After all, we were following a subsistence way of life surrounded by coconut trees on a tiny atoll in the middle of the massive Pacific Ocean. Having said that, watching the pupils march across Beru in all their finery and with such precision was quite a spectacle. The students definitely seemed to enjoy the occasion. I suppose it was an opportunity to take part in a special communal event, something the students always took great pleasure in and the islanders watching along the way also enjoyed!

The bokaboka ponds of Beru

The Queen's Birthday march across the causeway at Nuka - Jackie bringing up the rear on her bike

Chapter 11

Tarawa

As is often the case, a single mishap can often change the day-to-day running of our lives. This was certainly the case when Jackie's knee started to give her pain. After a day or two of discomfort, she found it difficult to walk and her knee was swelling.

Just like with my swollen hand, which was bitten by mosquitoes when we first arrived on Beru, we sought local advice. The consensus was that her knee would require a series of traditional massages. On this occasion, Rebika, the head teacher's wife, carried out the task. With her specially prepared coconut-oil concoction, she delicately and skilfully massaged Jackie's knee and repeated the treatment over a couple of additional sessions.

Unfortunately, unlike my hand, the knee didn't respond to treatment; either the cartilage or ligament in the knee must have been damaged in some way, which had resulted in fluid accumulating. Jackie was determined to carry on teaching her lessons, hobbling between our house and the classrooms and resting as much as she could, but the knee showed no signs of improvement.

We were fairly self-sufficient when it came to health matters; we had quite an extensive first-aid kit and Jackie had been building up her skills with her school dispensary. So far we had managed to stay healthy, even when Jackie developed an abscess on her gum. Working together with a needle and mirror, we pierced it, extracted the pus and cleaned her gum. Success! However, her knee wasn't improving.

After advice from the staff, we contacted the Beru Island Dresser, the equivalent of a nurse, who decided the fluid needed draining after which Jackie would require some antibiotics. The procedure was carried out and she began taking the tablets.

Jackie explained her predicament in one of her letters back to the UK:

At the moment I'm sitting outside on the veranda with my injured leg resting on the other chair. I'm now taking tetracycline but I still can't bend my leg. I have been told to simply sit here, listen to the waves breaking on the beach and rest!

Indeed, if anything her knee seemed to get worse and she developed little protruding white spots all over her body. Finally she followed her own advice to Sister Mary and was booked on the next flight to Tarawa. As luck would have it, our friend John was flying the plane and he took charge of Jackie when they landed on the main island. She stayed at his house and the following day Diana took Jackie to the hospital.

After a thorough examination, it was concluded that Jackie had reacted to the antibiotics. No further treatment was required apart from resting her leg and stopping the pills; within a few days, the knee should be back to its normal size.

Fortunately the school had a holiday shortly afterwards so I joined Jackie on the main island. When I arrived, her leg was indeed functioning properly so she could return to Beru. Unfortunately, I couldn't fly back on the same flight because of an outbreak of cholera on Tarawa, which had led to some travelling restrictions. I ended up returning to Beru a few days later.

Over the years, increasing numbers of people had been leaving the outer islands and moving to Tarawa with a dream of achieving a better life. As happens in many developing nations, they believed that living in the capital would help them find greater wealth and improved circumstances. Consequently, the population of Tarawa had been rising, especially in the Betio and Bairiki area of the atoll.

With more people living close together, very often in poor conditions, the struggling water system had become contaminated. Sewage had entered the water supply and infected many people: the 1977 cholera outbreak eventually caused 494 cases on the island but, thankfully, no fatalities. It was a very serious situation that required all those living on Tarawa to be extremely careful about hygiene, preparing food properly and making sure the water they used was free from the cholera bacteria.

After returning to Beru, I remember listening to Radio Tarawa's public health jingle, constantly being aired with accompanying catchy music: *'Drink boiled water, drink boiled water...'*

After a few months of vigilance, the cholera outbreak subsided but it was a warning shot across the bows for those living on the main island. Serious deliberations about water supply, sewage and over population were required if the cholera scare wasn't to be repeated. As the World Health Organisation pointed out:

The long-term solution for cholera control lies in economic development and universal access to safe drinking water and adequate sanitation.

Later in the year we were on Tarawa again, this time under more convivial circumstances. Jackie and I had arranged to produce some English teaching materials at the government-run King George V School, the main secondary school for the Gilbert Islands. It had more resources than our school and the teachers kindly allowed us to produce a number of English booklets using their school printing facilities.

Staff at KGV were quite happy with this arrangement as long as they also received a set of the materials, so we ran off extra copies and collated the pages. Co-operation and sharing resources in this way made a lot of sense for both establishments; after all, we were all working towards the same end – to help educate young people in this developing country.

It was always interesting strolling around Tarawa, an opportunity to get the feel of the place and compare it to Beru. One noticeable difference was the increase in the population. There were a number of shops rather than just one local island store and a greater variety of goods available for the larger numbers of people, including many foreigners who were working in the Gilberts.

Tarawa was the administrative hub of these islands, the centre of government; it had a palpable air of importance. There were quite a few cars and other vehicles on the road along the length of southern Tarawa, and there was also a minibus service! Jackie and I couldn't believe it when we first came across it. These vehicles could be hailed at stopping points, the white-washed bases of certain coconut trees.

We soon realised why many islanders were attracted to live in a more vibrant place. It had been suggested that VSOs at other locations around the developing world travel out of their designated country to have a break halfway through their tenure, but Jackie and I decided this wasn't for us: we decided to visit the 'hustle and bustle' of Tarawa.

As somebody who had toiled for many hours making our pig-pen on Beru, I was intrigued to see how they had been constructed on Tarawa. An American runway, which had been built rapidly during World War Two, had been broken up into sections by the local inhabitants. The pieces were reused to construct strong enclosures for their pigs. These perforated lengths of steel, known as Marston Matting, were originally slotted together to enable aircraft to take off and land.

The construction proved a significant factor in the American war effort. It was such a simple but remarkable invention whereby, for example, a 1500-metre runway could be constructed in under two days. Some thirty-plus years later, the Marston Matting had been put to another use ingeniously.

Walking around Betio, we saw a lot of evidence of the Battle of Tarawa, which took place in November 1943. This encounter was one of the bloodiest battles of the Pacific during the Second World War. All around were damaged concrete bunkers; war debris was exposed at low tide, including corroding machine guns. In one location stood a huge gun with a massive barrel still pointing out to sea.

During our time at Hiram Bingham High School, we saw a couple of students who had significant scars upon their faces. They told us that when they were children on Tarawa they had been victims of a popular game at the time. They had joined other young children searching in the sand around Betio for unexploded ordnance, a favourite being bullets. They used to take these treasures to old Japanese bunkers and throw them against the concrete walls. Some exploded, causing great glee, but some caused considerable damage and scarred unfortunate youngsters for the rest of their lives.

Seeing this war debris was a surprise so many years after the Battle of Tarawa. How the military on both sides of the conflict must have suffered and, of course, the population of the Gilbert Islands, especially those living on Tarawa. This foreign war, which had been imported to the islands, resulted in an invasion and the inhabitants were subjected to maltreatment and sometimes murder by their captors. For the Gilbert Islanders, it was a truly horrendous chapter.

This was also the case in the First World War when my grandfather, Frederick Green, died. Like many other young men of the period, he enlisted in the British Army at the outbreak of hostilities, and in September 1914 found himself fighting in France against the German forces. He became a driver in the Royal Field Artillery, skilfully riding horses pulling heavy guns into battle.

Fred was captured later that autumn and became a prisoner of war, eventually dying in December from his injuries. Visiting his grave in a military cemetery just outside Berlin was a poignant moment. Looking at row upon row of similar graves from my grandfather's graveside, I was staggered to see just how many lives had been lost. During the conflict, which has been dubbed 'The Great War', around 15 million people lost their lives. There had obviously also been a huge loss of life during the Second World War only two decades later!

The Japanese dropped their first bombs in the Gilbert Islands on December 8th 1941 on the phosphate-rich island of Banaba to the west. The following day, Japanese troops occupied the northern islands of Makin, Butaritari, Abaiang and Marakei. They also arrived on Tarawa, which the commanders recognised as a strategic location.

The Japanese decided to build their headquarters on the islet of Betio at the western tip of the atoll. So began the formidable task of turning it into a fortress, with the sole aim of stopping the advance of American forces as they pushed westwards across the Pacific towards Japan. Consequently, all the Betio fortifications needed to be carefully constructed upon this thin triangular-shaped islet measuring just three kilometres long by not even a kilometre wide.

Local men from Tarawa and Abaiang were forced to work on these fortifications together with the Japanese military and Korean labourers who had arrived as part of the invasion force. They built concrete emplacements for guns of all sizes, communication stations and fortified bunkers, as well as tank traps and underwater mines. Coconut trees from across many islands were felled, cut into logs and taken to Betio to reinforce these defences. They dug a network of trenches to enable troops to move around unseen if the Americans arrived.

The Japanese had planned their stay on the island carefully and brought in masses of food supplies, bicycles, motorcycles, cars and trucks. Included in the construction detail was a 500m-long pier jutting out from the north shore to enable supply ships to offload supplies. Finally, a runway was constructed running east to west down the centre of Betio.

The Gilbertese workforce feared the Japanese, who beat them if they didn't work hard enough. It was tiring work carrying rocks, digging holes and hauling heavy construction material. There was no pay, just a little food – which was always rice. The Betio stronghold took almost a year to build and required a massive effort to complete; when finished, the Japanese military were satisfied with their work.

The project needed a phenomenal amount of local and imported materials. As an onlooker during the 1970s, I could only speculate what might have been achieved if such human effort and vast resources had been put to more constructive and positive use!

Inspecting the completed fortress on Betio, Rear Admiral Shibazaki of Japan confidently proclaimed to his men:

'It would take one million men one hundred years to conquer Tarawa!'

In time, a large American invasion force sailed towards the Gilbert Islands on aircraft carriers, battleships, cruisers, destroyers and transport ships with thousands of military personnel onboard. The fighting force started their attack by bombarding Betio by ship and by air for three days before sending in troops. However, this onslaught didn't weaken the Japanese positions because their fortress was capable of withstanding much of the bombardment.

At dawn on the 20th of November 1943, the first of three waves of troops moved to shore. Due to a miscalculation of the tide depth, most of the landing craft were unable to take the marines onto the beaches as they required a minimum clearance of 1.2 metres to get over the coral reef. On the day, there was only a clearance of 0.9 metres in what was a neap tide.

This serious mistake resulted in the troops having to wade about 500 metres to shore with their heavy equipment and weaponry. The situation was described by Robert Sherrod in his book entitled *Tarawa – the Story of a Battle*:

No sooner had we hit the water than the Japanese machine guns really opened up on us… It was painfully slow, wading in such deep water. And we had seven hundred yards to walk slowly into that machine-gun fire… I was scared, as I had never been scared before.

The error resulted in many Americans being easy targets for the Japanese to fire upon. Hundreds of marines, as many as 70% of the initial wave, lost their lives. Once ashore, the fighting was intense, with the might of both the Japanese and American forces engaged in a full-blown, bloody battle using heavy guns, machine guns, tanks, flame-throwers, mortars, a range of firearms, grenades and other weaponry.

As well as land forces, there was firepower from battleships and war planes. On the second day, the Americans started to gain the upper hand even though the Japanese put up strong resistance, not least from individual snipers. By the end of day three, the Americans had taken control of Betio.

One reason why the invasion was slower than anticipated was because of the unexpectedly strong fortifications on the island. After inspecting one of the bunkers after the battle, Sherrod explained why the American bombardment had such difficulty penetrating the Japanese defences:

Double thickness of eight-inch-thick coconut logs, hooked together with steel spikes, buttressed by upright logs driven into the ground, covered by three feet of shrapnel-absorbing sand.

At the end of the Battle of Tarawa almost 6,400 Japanese, American and Koreans had died in fighting which lasted some seventy-six hours! When hostilities ceased, Sherrod, who was a war correspondent during the battle, concluded:

What I saw on Betio was, I am certain, one of the greatest works of devastation wrought by man.

As soon as the Japanese had invaded the Gilberts, the islands became more isolated from the world. Those living on the northern atolls, who had more dealings with the Japanese, often suffered far more than those living on the southern islands where there was not a lot of contact.

Although the Japanese didn't occupy all of the islands, they did visit them and raised the Japanese flag when they arrived. The Gilbertese on these outer islands were given orders to follow, which were checked on future visits.

One of the most noticeable changes to the islanders' lives was that trading ships stopped calling at the Gilbert Islands, and imported items such as cloth, tobacco and kerosene soon ran out. To solve the problem, people made do with food they could grow, karewe they could cut, and fish they could catch. In other words, they continued living their traditional subsistence lifestyle.

There were many stories of cruelty and disruption where the Japanese soldiers were stationed, but there were also instances of kindness. In *A History of Kiribati*, Michael Walsh wrote:

Although ... 780 Gilbertese and Ellice Islanders lost their lives during World War Two ... they were mostly bystanders.

There was a heavy loss of life in the colony during this period considering that they were not the instigators of such hostilities.

After the Battle of Tarawa, the Americans helped the local islanders rebuild their lives. There were a great number of tasks to be carried out, particularly on South Tarawa. Betio needed to be reconstructed, many village homes throughout Tarawa were in ruins, people had been displaced and, most essential to island subsistence, around 60,000 coconut trees had been either chopped down or destroyed during the battle.

One of the most immediate concerns, however, was the lack of food: people were starving. To alleviate this problem, the local islanders were provided with American rations; they were also paid well if they worked on reconstruction projects.

After such awful experiences during the years of occupation, followed by the battle itself, there must have been a collective feeling of relief. Indeed, the Americans were so popular that some opposition to the return of British rule developed. The people of North Tarawa were so happy with their new liberators that 200 people signed a petition asking to be permanently under the control of the United States. However, their plea came to nothing; when the last American troops left in 1946, the Gilbert Islands returned to British colonial rule.

Things were never quite the same, though; people had experienced great trauma and been exposed to a different way of life. By the 1950s, Tarawa had become the commercial, administrative, medical and educational centre of the island and replaced the pre-war island of Banaba as the new capital. As a consequence, Tarawa developed more quickly than other Gilbertese islands. The importance of the island is reflected in the way the population of South Tarawa grew from 1,643 in 1947 to 17,000 in 1977.

Just like other colonies across the world, the seeds of independence had been sown during and after World War Two. Tarawa was the location where such changes would, in time, come to fruition.

*'The Battle of Tarawa', a painting by Sergeant Tom Lovell,
United States Marine Corps*

Betio on Tarawa, the focus of the fighting
Courtesy of the Imperial War Museum

During the 1970s, there was still a great deal of evidence of the Battle of Tarawa

The Battle of Tarawa – Courtesy: Imperial War Museum

Chapter 12

Back at School

Back on Beru, life continued as Jackie and I worked through the school year. Foremost amongst our tasks at Rongorongo was to teach English to students and we were always thinking of different ways to develop their skills.

Understanding and using an unfamiliar foreign medium wasn't always easy for the students; this was their second language with a host of strange sounds and written words as well as complicated rules of grammar to contend with. However, as with other subject areas within school, all the pupils were keen to learn. By and large there was a collective desire to make a success of any opportunities that were presented to them.

Using our limited English teaching resources, we attempted to develop pupils' oral, aural, reading and writing skills. The teaching materials we used had to be chosen carefully so our pupils with their atoll life could appreciate them. Using English resources with more 'developed-world' scenarios invariably caused confusion, and lessons could be dominated by explaining cultural aspects rather than using them for developing English.

An aspect of teaching that often produced positive results, was when we were developing oral skills and encouraging pupils to speak the language. We began with the experiences of the students and worked outwards from there.

One example was when I asked students to explain stories and legends from the islands. After they had told the story, I would ask them to write it down – the most challenging aspect of any language. It was made easier because the students were familiar with the stories.

An example of this was when one second-year pupil retold the Gilbertese legend of *Nei Kuiku*. It is about a girl who travelled all the way to the moon and helped a blind woman see again. First, groups of students acted out the legend, translating it into English as they went along, then wrote the story. (Some sections of their tale have been missed out.)

Once upon a time, on the island of Nabanaba, there lived a woman whose name was Nei Kuiku. She had three daughters. Their names were first Nei Kuiku, second Nei Kuiku and third Nei Kuiku... The third or youngest Nei Kuiku went to the beach ... and turned over coconut shells... She found a plant which could grow to the moon.... Nei Kuiku climbed up to the moon... There she found an old woman who was blind... Nei Kuiku told the old woman that she would blow the dust away from her eyes, which she did... The old woman could see again... The old woman's three sons were very happy... In the end Nei Kuiku was married to the youngest son and they both lived happily ever after.

When this story was eventually completed, it was included in *Sunrise*, the Hiram Bingham High School magazine that we had started. This school publication encouraged students to put their own work into print so other pupils, family members and friends could read their work.

Eventually, pupils were able to invent original stories, working individually or in groups. This was a greater challenge because it required a more creative process, but it was an opportunity to use ideas gleaned from outside sources such as novels.

On more than one occasion we produced short plays of their work, complete with simple costumes and props, and performed them on stage in the school hall. Whenever possible, we taught the mechanics of English through such oral exercises whilst studying suitable reading materials. A certain amount of teaching used 'chalk and blackboard' explanations, but over time we saw progress in almost all pupils' ability to use English.

It was important to be adaptable and prepared for timetable adjustments. There was one occasion at Rongorongo when we only had six teaching staff instead of twelve! Rikameta was away in Fiji, so Tametra, Jackie and I had to come up with a new timetable during a weekend. This interim timetable included essential subjects and explored a few new aspects of the curriculum, but the six remaining members of staff had to work extra hours throughout this period.

One alteration was that I started teaching geography to some pupils. We studied the Gilbert Islands and nearby Pacific nations, which gave us the opportunity to look at the physical attributes of our neighbours.

Interestingly, there was a Stephenson screen weather station in school, most of which was still functioning, so students spent a month taking meteorological readings, studying the weather and climate of the region and recording wind direction, rainfall and the type of weather for each day.

It turned out to be a useful study of a location that sometimes suffered from drought and relied on regular rainfall to top up the groundwater that naturally accumulated beneath the atolls. Such freshwater, accessed by wells, rests on top of the denser saline water beneath it. This unique natural process is of paramount importance for those living on an atoll; when the freshwater becomes too depleted, people cannot drink the salty water below.

On Beru, the villages relied almost exclusively on this underground 'freshwater lens', as it is known, without which the island would have been uninhabitable. It is a remarkable and delicate phenomena of atolls. Our weather study results were also included in the school magazine.

During periods of rain, it was fascinating to observe the shower clouds heading for Beru. Just before rain arrived, there would be a noticeable gust of wind that blew vigorously across the island to warn us of an impending deluge. Being open to the ocean, these pre-shower winds were always noticeable. When the rain eventually arrived, it could fall exceptionally heavily. There were times when it was so torrential that pupils would race outside from their dormitories and stand under downpipes with their soap to enjoy a warm shower!

English was the medium central to all teaching at Hiram Bingham High School. Whatever the subject, be it mathematics, science or religious studies, it was taught in English. For example, in social studies there were numerous resource materials in English that had been produced by the University of the South Pacific in Fiji. Work involved reading, discussions and invariably writing, so English skills were being reinforced across the curriculum. These studies examined the more human aspects of life all across the Pacific region. This example is from a social studies unit where second year pupils were asked the question: *'You are a Minister of Tourism. What do you think about tourism? Is it a good thing or a bad thing?'*

The students discussed the pros and cons of tourism in groups, something of a challenge for them because there was practically no tourism in the Gilbert Islands, unlike Fiji, Samoa or Tonga. However, there were foreign visitors to the Gilberts who were employed by the government, churches and agencies (like VSO), so pupils could make judgements on what contacts they had experienced with foreigners. After their discussion, they were asked to write up their conclusions:

Tourism is a good thing for we get lots of money from it. If there are tourists there are more hotels to be built, more workers are wanted, local dancing is revived so they will know what our traditional dancing is... Our handicrafts are bought by them so we get more money... It is also a good thing for we will learn more English and other languages... When our copra is not wanted ... when the phosphate is finished tourism can replace it

On the other hand, some pupils argued:

It is a bad thing to introduce tourism ... our people will see it and follow it e.g. try to wear foreign clothes. In our custom we wear very long dresses and men wear lavalavas. Tourists have also introduced their bad manners and behaviour ... they walk in front of houses and don't think of the people inside... Tourists and people from overseas have brought bad diseases, which spread everywhere. They also throw rubbish everywhere.

Social studies were always informative, thought provoking and provided interesting discussions. Work from our units was occasionally displayed in the school hall for others to read and hopefully comment on.

Another social studies unit looked at housing in the Pacific Islands. This fascinating study looked at the differences in traditional home building between Tonga, Samoa and Fiji, islands which have some elevation, and the atoll locations of the Ellice and Gilbert Islands which were basically flat. The type of island historically determined the design and materials used in the construction of traditional homes.

I greatly admired how the people of the Gilbert Islands manage to live successfully on 'one-dimensional islands', islands with practically no elevation or width, just long lines in the ocean.

One boy in school wrote a detailed outline of how his family built a new home:

My father decided to build a new house for our family and relations...When they were in the bush my father told people which trees they should cut down...When the trunks were all in the village the men started to dig holes for the poles ... they put the poles in six holes... they put other sticks on the poles... children went and fetched leaves from the women...They put the roof on and tied it with string... My father put the leaves on... My mother and the other women worked hard weaving the leaves and mats...When the mats were finished they put them on the floor of the new house.

As well as learning about aspects of neighbouring Pacific regions, we studied specific Gilbertese topics of interest. One such study focussed on the Battle of Tarawa, which was pertinent to the lives of many of the students.

As in other educational establishments around the world, formal assessments took place usually as the school year came to a close. Some of these exams took place in the school hall with teachers invigilating. When the exams were completed, the teachers had to knuckle down and complete the marking.

I remember overseeing one exam in the hall when I was given a mug of tea together with a couple of heavily sugared donuts (staff were treated well during such sessions!). Unfortunately, I forgot about these as I went around the hall watching the pupils.

At the end of the exam, the students left their test papers on their tables and went off to their dorms. As I collected the papers, I noticed a long line of ants, hundreds of them, walking purposefully across the floor. Some were going in one direction, others were walking the opposite way.

I followed the line and discovered it stopped at the tin plate on which the donuts had been placed. The ants were, bit by bit, carrying the individual sugar crystals out of the hall and disappearing into some bushes – quite amazing!

Teachers were required to carry out certain professional duties at Hiram Bingham High School, including evening sessions where we supervised students' homework. This usually took place in one of the classrooms. If the school generator was working it was fine; pupils could work for an hour and, if they finished, they would read a book. However, if the generator was out of action, a frequent occurrence, completing homework was more problematic as the students had to rely on pressure lamps to complete their writing and reading. With their half-sphere metallic bases containing kerosene, a pump at the side would be vigorously pumped up in order to increase the pressure enabling the light above to shine. The more you pumped, the brighter the light. With the best will in the world, such lamps didn't produce the light provided by electricity no matter how much you pumped up the pressure, and we often had pupils complaining of aching eyes.

Similarly, Jackie and I found it challenging when we marked pupils' work, wrote or read by pressure lamp during the evening.

There was another school activity where girls at Rongorongo were obliged to make coconut string, a tradition in the islands carried out by girls and women. Female members of staff supervised this task and it was completed by girls sitting upon the ground. Coconut fibres were rolled and twisted on a person's thigh until they had a long length. It was always fascinating to watch. This string was used for many, many jobs so you could never have enough of it. Once the lengths were completed, they were stored away ready to be used as and when required.

As far as teaching duties went, my personal favourite was overseeing the evening meal in the school mess room a few minutes away from our house. This wasn't because delicious food was provided for the students; the duty staff would sample it before it was served and it was invariably some kind of fish and rice. To be honest, it was often not very tasty. No, I didn't look forward to the eating experience but to the whole event.

Before the famished children were given the go-ahead to eat, they had to sing grace. Gilbertese singing is arguably some of the most harmonious on the planet; although I am no expert, I think the islanders' ability to sing in four-part harmony is quite sublime. I would have a couple of minutes of extreme pleasure while the students sang; their rendition was simply magical and sent shivers down my spine!

If that wasn't extraordinary enough, it always took place at the end of the day just as the sun was setting. The combination of exquisite harmonies against a backdrop of a purple, red and orange sky with a silhouette of tropical trees was the most precious of moments. I must admit, there were occasions when I complained that their singing wasn't up to their usual standard (untrue, of course!) so they had to sing it one more time. I would be faced by a sea of surprised faces because their singing was always perfect, but they always obliged. Oh joy!

Jackie and I were in charge of the school library. After being at the school for more than a year, we decided to apply for a grant from the British Council for new library books. In the salty and damp atoll atmosphere, books often suffered. Pupils enjoyed the ones that were available and were encouraged to take away, read and share them with others in their dormitories, so they were well used but did become a little tired looking.

The British Council informed us that we could spend a considerable amount of money on new books. Brilliant! After receiving a number of book catalogues, we took great care in selecting a range of fiction and non-fiction titles. This wasn't as easy as it might seem because we didn't want any of them to be too challenging for the students. The aim was to develop a joy in reading, not turn them off with unappealing content. We wanted books that would inform, amuse and absorb the youngsters. Ideally, we also didn't want any of them to be too culturally overpowering.

Sadly we came across very few titles that reflected life in the Pacific islands, but eventually we chose the books and sent the long list of titles to the British Council. Weeks later, the boxes arrived.

The next stage involved reorganising the library to accommodate the new volumes. With help from some of the students, the books were housed on spruced-up shelves.

We all had fun looking through these new titles; Jackie spent a lot of time reading a series of cartoon books of *The Adventures of Tintin*. When it was time to re-open the library, the volumes were soon being used and enjoyed.

Towards the end of the school year, there was a Sports Day for the students. For a school located just one degree south of the Equator, this wasn't ideal in many ways. With temperatures hovering around 30°C all year long, pupils getting overheated was a concern. Also, a Sports Day was a new idea, not a tradition at the school. With next to no sports' equipment, we would have to be creative.

The staff came up with a few suggestions that we thought might work and, after some deliberation, we were ready. Staff members would organise the events, record results and resolve any problems that occurred. The students were encouraged to take part in as many activities as possible. There would be sports for both girls and boys, as well as some activities exclusively for each gender.

To start the day, girls and boys took part in separate kung-fu displays, an activity that was regularly practised during sport sessions. Each performance involved arm punching, jumping and other superbly demonstrated muscular movements; it was an impressive, synchronised exhibition.

Next, there was a high jump competition for boys only. This was a magnificent display of their ability to leap over ever-increasing heights. They hadn't really practised the skills required to jump to such heights, but they worked out what was needed. At the highest point, they placed their limbs precisely so their bodies curved over the bar without dislodging it.

The girls then competed to see who could throw a husked coconut the furthest, a little like shot-put but with a bigger object. They could only use one arm, so it wasn't easy.

Next, the girls competed to see who could weave a traditional Gilbertese ball the quickest using a number of pandanus leaf strands. The quality of the finished balls was also taken into consideration. The girls stood alongside each other, concentrating hard as their nimble fingers wove away.

For the boys, there was a series of tug-of-war competitions to test their individual strength and collective brawn. Both girls and boys competed to find out who could take the husk off a coconut the fastest – the most useful of island skills – using a traditional pointed wooden husker or *te koro*. At the end of the competition, piles of coconut husks and coconuts littered the ground, providing a mass of supplies for the school cooks: husks to be burnt as fuel and coconuts to be used with meals!

The sports day finale consisted of races for each sex around a set course. Unfortunately, by the time these took place the sun was at its highest. To make it harder, students were running barefoot over sand, sharp coral stones and grass that sometimes contained little thorns that stuck to the soles of their feet. Even so, everybody had a lot of fun – so much so that at the end of the event some students elected to run with another person on their back – a 'piggy-back' race.

The morning was a huge success. When they were not competing, the pupils sat in the shade of the trees and were enthusiastic spectators, eagerly supporting their friends.

The event showed how strong and capable these girls and boys of the Pacific Islands were. They were natural athletes and worked out how best to perform to best effect with hardly any training.

For me, who spent every other day attempting to stay fit by running my route across the beach and leaping over obstacles in the bush, it was very impressive. I had to work hard to stay slightly fit whereas these young islanders appeared to be naturals. Quite incredible!

Sports Day: 'Throwing the coconut'

Sports Day: 'Kung Fu'

Sports Day: 'Kung Ku'

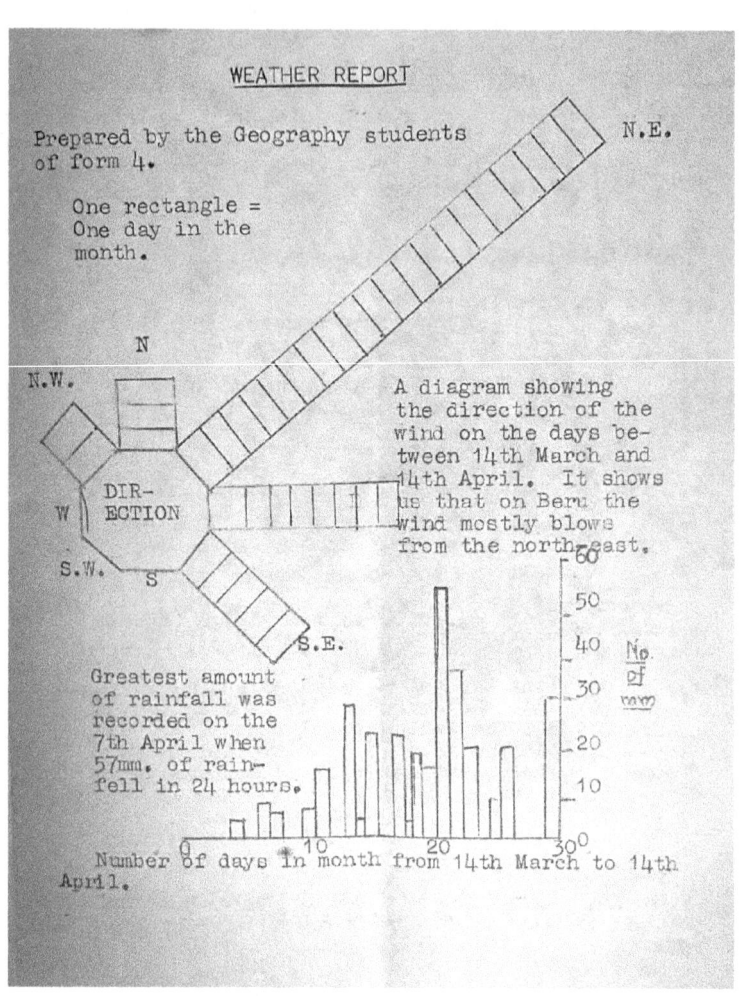

'Our weather study' by Form 4

'These are our Gilbert Islands' by Forms 1P and 1F

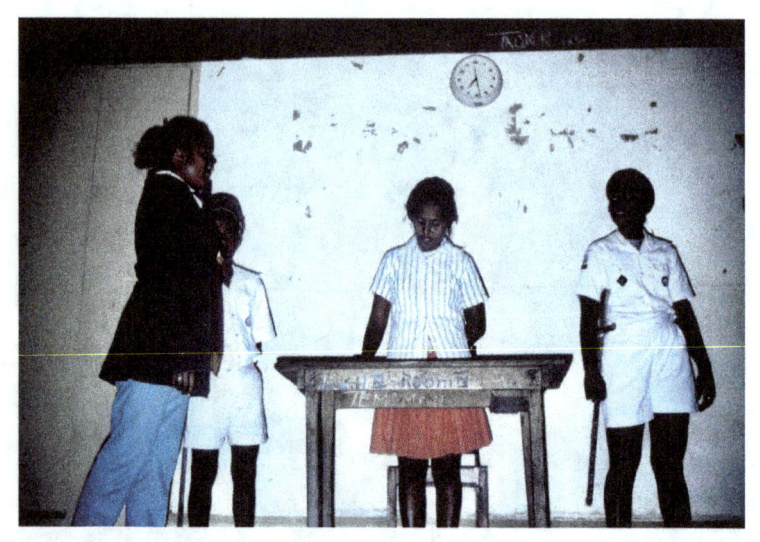

A short play being written and performed by the pupils

Work completed by Form 3 about the War in the Pacific

Sports Day: 'High jump'

The school library

Chapter 13

A New Maneaba and Visitors to Beru

During our time at Hiram Bingham High School, the village had to decide whether to build a new maneaba on the campus. In any settlement in the Gilbert Islands, this is a significant event; not only is a maneaba the most prominent structure in a village, traditionally it is also the focal point of the community. These tall, wide, steep-sided buildings have a special atmosphere; they stand like South-Sea island pyramids and enjoy a similar majesty over their flat surroundings.

Certain traditions and formalities are carried out in the maneaba and it is a place of ancestral importance. Over time, it has evolved to become a place where decisions are agreed upon by the community for those within the community. A certain etiquette is expected of those who sit in this somewhat revered building.

Although our Rongorongo maneaba was a school-based building, traditions and formalities were still observed whenever ceremonies, feasts, dances and social events took place. It was where visitors were formally welcomed, people honoured when they were leaving, where important meetings occurred and religious events were performed, as well as being a location for our Saturday school gatherings. It was also where the school staff might share a meal and enjoy some time together, particularly on Sundays and during religious festivals.

As with other local buildings, a maneaba is made entirely from natural resources: coconut and pandanus timber; thatch made of pandanus and, rather amazingly, all held together by wooden pegs and endless metres of coconut string. It is, indeed, an architectural wonder!

According to island history, the very first maneaba ever built in the Gilbert Islands was during the 1400s on the atoll of Beru. Following a feud in the Polynesian islands of Samoa to the southeast, a Samoan man named Tematawarebwe and his followers fled to the Gilbert Islands.

After a long ocean journey, they eventually landed at the southern end of Beru where they settled. Using their Polynesian building skills, the migrants built a maneaba-style meeting house, similar to ones they had in Samoa. This first maneaba was built in the village of Tebontebike on Beru; over time, similar village meeting houses were constructed across the Gilbert Islands.

Eventually societal rules and governance were formulated through collective agreement during village meetings within the *maneaba*. As Sister Alaina Talu and Frances Tekonnang wrote in *Kiribati – Aspects of History*:

The maneaba has always been the centre of Gilbertese social life. It is where the villagers meet to discuss all matters of importance pertaining to village life.

If disputes occurred on the islands, they were dealt with during maneaba meetings. In an environment with limited resources, it was essential that village members lived in harmony. The formula that appeared to work most of the time – although some disputes must have failed considering the number of warlike battles that occasionally peppered the islands' history!

A system evolved within the maneaba whereby particular family groups (*kaainga*) were allotted certain sitting positions around its edge, known as *boti*. These were not to be used by outsiders. The boti system meant that a person journeying to a different island would be allowed to sit in an unfamiliar maneaba at the place of their extended family or kaainga. Thus any islander could travel through the Gilbert Islands and find distant family to welcome them.

Nakibae Tabokai, writing in *Atoll Politics*, sums up the importance of the Gilbertese maneaba:

...the maneaba in Kiribati (Gilbertese) tradition is something special. It symbolises the ultimate reality of life for the people on the islands. It stands as the house of justice and the house of entertainment and accommodation. In addition, each **kaainga**

has its own sitting position in the maneaba called the *boti*, thus every individual has a place in the maneaba.

Traditionally, building a maneaba involved all members of the village. Everybody would take part in its construction in some way, contributing string and thatch, tree-cutting, weaving or labour. Both sexes and the older children helped to build it.

Marita Davies in the Melbourne Museum's *'Tok Stori Vikitolia Pacific'* interviews, commented:

...even though it's the men's role to build the structure ... it can't be built without women making the string ... literally holding together the community...

With every villager contributing to the building, the new maneaba would belong to all of them. No single person's contribution was more important than another person's. What is also fascinating is that a traditional maneaba construction involves intricate building skills that evolved over time, such as understanding which knots to use and how to tie them when fixing timber beams together.

Considering the height of the building, the weight of the wood and the awkward positions of the knots, the construction did indeed require specialist skills.

There were also age-old rituals and 'magic' that had to be performed at particular times during its construction. If these traditions were not adhered to, the maneaba spirits might become upset and that put the success of the construction at risk.

With most of the wood prepared, specialist constructors at hand, the thatch and string makers busy and the correct ritual words ready, the old maneaba was taken down and it was time to build our new school maneaba. Jackie and I were busy teaching, so we could not witness every stage of the process but we went along as often as we could to watch its progress.

The site was a hive of activity and the speed of construction was impressive. Holes were dug and the upright poles were secured into place, then the cross beams pegged and tied into position to make the high sloping roof. This was heavy work involving a range of precarious positions for the men involved, another example of natural Pacific athleticism. How on earth they got themselves into such complex positions then secured heavy pieces of wood and tied intricate knots using coconut string was beyond me. Years of climbing coconut trees to collect karewe must have helped hone the required skills.

As always, they climbed in bare feet wearing only shorts or a wraparound lavalava. If any sawing was required, no matter how hefty or how long the timber was it was done entirely by hand. There were no mechanical tools and no safety equipment. We had never seen some of the men who were clambering upon the poles and beams before; men who were linked to the church and possessed the required building skills had been brought in from neighbouring villages.

Soon, the pandanus thatch was ready to be secured onto the roof with string. Most of the Rongorongo women had steadily been producing lengths of thatch during the weeks before the start of building. Great quantities of string were required for every stage of the building process and this had been produced by the girls in school and the female members of staff. It had involved countless hours of sitting down skilfully weaving lengths of thatch as well as delicately rolling quantities of string upon their thighs.

A key personality was Aire, our school carpenter. He supervised the whole process and had a precise vision of how the maneaba construction should take place.

Impressively, within a few weeks the building was finished; naturally, there was then a formal opening ceremony with speeches, feasting and dancing for the whole school.

Beru felt very remote during our two years on the island, unlike Tarawa, the main island, where there were continually visitors arriving for a variety of reasons. As the capital of the colony, people were bound to visit especially as the islands transitioned towards independence.

By 1977, the Gilberts had reached the initial stages on this journey and achieved internal self-government. The Gilbertese were gradually taking control of different government departments and getting to grips with the skills they needed to take charge of their destiny. But, as I previously explained, few visitors ever ventured onto the outer islands with their subsistence way of living and traditional lifestyle.

Having said that, during our time on Beru we did encounter a number of people. As our island was the location for one of the nation's three secondary schools, many of our visitors were linked to the school or the church.

American missionaries from the United States, Jim and Alice, were in Australia before they came to the islands. Fortunately Jim was a teacher and joined our staff – if a person can teach, get them on the timetable!

They lived with their three children on the lagoon side of Rongorongo in another missionary house, which had the largest breadfruit tree we'd ever seen growing outside.

Alice and Jim admitted that living on Beru was a great contrast to their lives in Australia, where they had also been involved with missionary work; they admitted that their Australian experience had not been dissimilar to their previous lives in Chicago. Living in the Gilbert Islands was more challenging, with limited resources and few modern facilities.

A fascinating element of their stay was the way their three children made progress in speaking Gilbertese. These youngsters – a boy aged eleven, a girl aged seven and a boy of four – eventually acquired the language level that corresponded almost exactly to the predominant theories of language acquisition.

After a few months on the island, just as the family were leaving Beru, the eldest boy had learnt hardly any of the local language, the daughter had learnt a smattering, but the youngest boy was fluent. Was this evidence that, as humans, we have the greatest capacity to learn a language the younger we are? I realise this wasn't a proper scientific 'Noam Chomsky' style study, but even so it was rather interesting.

Towards the end of our stay, John and Kateta came to Hiram Bingham High School. Kateta, who was Gilbertese, had married John from Britain and they had been living in New Zealand. They were also connected to the church and John joined the teaching staff.

Other visitors included teachers from the King George V School, the government secondary school on Tarawa. They came to see what life was like on an outer island and took the opportunity to look around a different secondary school. There was also Howard, who worked for the University of the South Pacific, who came to stay with us for a few days, and Diana, our pilot's wife, who wanted to experience life on Beru.

These occasional visits broke up our time on the island, provided different characters to chat to and show around our school, and added a little spice to our lives.

Possibly one of the most bizarre visits was one which lasted no more than several minutes! A young British official flew in on the small inter-island plane. After taxiing to a halt, he asked the pilot to wait and not leave without him. He commandeered our island police officer to take him to our school, where we met him standing outside our house one lunchtime immaculately dressed in white shirt, shorts and socks.

He spoke to Jackie:

'Hello. Are you Jackie? I have brought this small package for you. Inside you will find the items you requested.'

With that, the young man leapt on the back of the motor-bike and sped off. He was obviously in a hurry to catch the plane waiting for him.

When we looked inside the parcel, there were packets of contraception pills! Jackie had informed VSO that she was running low so, not wishing to increase the population of Beru, they had sent a government official with a special delivery. Such a great service, for which we were both very grateful!

One of the most significant visits for the whole island during our stay was from five New Zealanders who came as part of an aid project with the aim of creating a bigger passage through the reef. This would allow inter-island vessels to dock more easily when delivering goods and transporting passengers.

These antipodean specialists brought an array of equipment including a mechanical digger, heavy lifting gear, a Jeep and boxes of sundry items that included a quantity of explosives. The robust, no-nonsense Kiwis spent a couple of weeks on Beru. The highlight of their visit was when explosives were used to blast through the coral reef. Word had spread through the islands that we should prepare for a feast when this took place.

On the days when detonations occurred in the far north of Beru where the ships tied up, people were ready. Everyone kept well clear of any explosions but then waited and looked out to sea because the blasts killed hundreds of fish and other marine creatures! Free food was literally scooped out of the water whenever the 'all clear' was given. It was a huge New Zealand gift to the islanders, which made every villager on Beru exceedingly happy.

During the reef blasters' stay, Jackie and I invited them to our house for food one evening. They arrived in their Jeep then drove across the school grounds, causing an almighty commotion amongst the pupils and staff on the Rongorongo campus. We were not used to seeing vehicles on the island; there was one small government-owned truck that was seen occasionally in various parts of Beru – but a Jeep in our school? With a whole load of New Zealand I-Matang?

We had done our best to produce enough food for our guests: fish, coconuts, breadfruit and rice. However, we needn't have worried because they brought an assortment of edible goodies, including a case of Kiwi beer.

This particular New Zealand aid project was a definite success. As well as blasting passages in outer island reefs, wherever they arrived, they created a wake of cheer in many ways for many people.

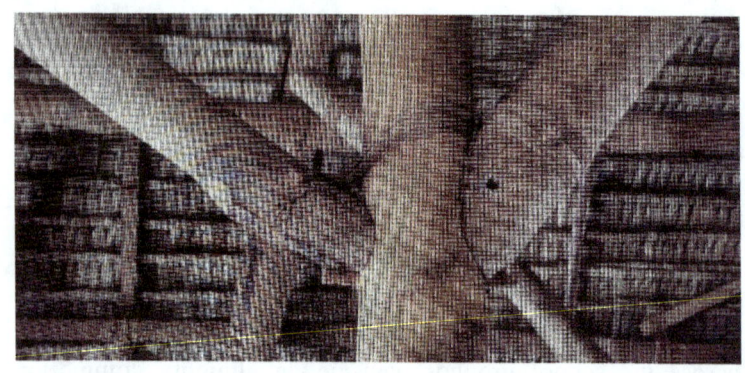

Maneaba beams are joined by using string, knots and wooden pegs – Courtesy Tony Whincup

A maneaba on the island of Arorae

The maneaba string and knots hold up the entire structure
Courtesy: Tony Whincup

School pupils standing on the New Zealand bulldozer

The building of the new maneaba at Rongorongo

Constructing the new school maneaba

Chapter 14

Our Final Days on Beru

The date for our departure was approaching rapidly and the final few weeks seemed to fly past as we prepared to leave. But we were not on our way just yet.

In the last weeks of working at Hiram Bingham High School, Jackie was invited to dance during one of the Saturday night gatherings in the school maneaba. The plan was to perform a traditional dance with Kateta, John's Gilbertese wife, who had arrived on Beru after living in New Zealand.

The request terrified my good wife. A traditional Gilbertese dance in front of the entire school? No way! It reminded us of when we first arrived on Tarawa and were asked to give a speech in the local maneaba. Such public displays weren't something either of us were used to, but during our time in the islands we had given a number of speeches and even sung a few traditional Scottish and Irish songs during maneaba gatherings. We now felt reasonably comfortable doing that – but dancing was another matter!

Not wanting to offend either pupils or staff, Jackie reluctantly agreed. Besides, it would be a suitable farewell gesture, a dance of friendship and appreciation. When Jackie found out that she and Kateta would receive special tuition, it softened the blow a little; any guidance would be gratefully received.

On the afternoon of the first rehearsal, Jackie went off to find Kateta, after which they met up with their dance tutor. Only the best traditional dance teacher on the island would do for these two ladies! She was an old woman from nearby Nuka village who unfortunately spoke no English, which meant that Kateta was burdened with constant translation.

Jackie returned from her first lesson several hours later looking despondent.

'How did the dancing go? Good fun?' I enquired.

'It was awful! I'm useless! There's no way I'm going to be able to learn this dance!' she lamented.

To perform a traditional Gilbertese dance was a difficult ask for any I-Matang; it wasn't part of our cultural experience, with all the nuances entwined into the psyche of an islander required for such a performance. All Gilbertese are exposed to traditional dancing skills throughout their lives and they can tap into a vast array of knowledge and references, both consciously and subconsciously. I suppose it's similar to how I had struggled with local fishing techniques and my first attempts at cutting karewe, which were disastrous.

However, Jackie pressed ahead; she wouldn't be beaten. During the following rehearsals, she was taught how to hold outstretched arms, make bird-like movements, move her hips correctly and to use her eyes appropriately, all while following the rhythm of the singing.

Kateta relayed essential instructions to Jackie, though this wasn't easy for her because, despite being Gilbertese, she had married an I-Matang and been absorbed into a faraway culture. She feared she might have forgotten the required skills, but it didn't take long to re-awaken her dormant abilities.

Their elderly tutor had an unforgiving way of using a stick to nudge, poke and tap particular parts of their anatomy. Jackie stopped requiring any translation and soon learned the woman's words, facial expressions and tones of displeasure. Wielding a stick was a great way of encouraging improvement! The experience for both women was exhausting but there were definite signs of progress.

When Jackie returned from her final practice, she had a smile on her face.

'How was the dancing? Are you both ready for tomorrow's performance?' I enquired.

'Yes, I think we are, though I was still having problems with my hips. They just aren't swinging enough – but we managed to solve the problem.'

'How?'

'I'm going to wear an extra grass skirt. Wearing two, my hip movement is much better!' she exclaimed gleefully.

With Jackie's hips sorted out, she was all set for the big day. On Saturday evening the school settled into the maneaba and the proceedings began. Finally Jackie and Kateta took their positions and there was a buzz of anticipation as the women prepared themselves. They were wearing grass skirts, white tibuta tops and colourful body sashes, with impressive woven garlands on their hair, and delicate arm bands. Their faces showed no emotion as they entered a pre-performance state.

They looked spectacular. It was easy to see why many islanders thought Jackie to be part-Gilbertese: after many months of Pacific sunshine, she was bronzed, had dark hair to below her waist and her physical features were not dissimilar to those of local island women.

The singing began with a single voice followed by the entire maneaba's rhythmic and somewhat chant-like accompaniment, then the dancers began to interpret the song with the appropriate gestures learned during their numerous lessons. The movements had to be precise as dictated by tradition.

It was a joy to watch Jackie perform. She had been privileged to be allowed into some of the secrets of the islands and her movements were superb. As they danced, and as custom prescribed, somebody produced talcum powder and liberally showered them both as a sign of approval. They ignored the white powder; their focus was totally on their dance. As was often the case during such dancing, the atmosphere was electric, the singing was in perfect four-part harmony and all those within the maneaba became one. 'Maneaba magic' had tapped into all our souls.

When the dance ended there was applause from the entire school – not least from Jackie's proud husband!

Not long afterwards, a wedding took place in school between two relatively new members of the staff: Betero, who mainly taught maths and some science, and Temonari who taught science.

As preparations got underway, we discovered that the couple needed a pig for the wedding feast so Jackie and I offered them our bush pig, Ezmeralda. As we were leaving Rongorongo soon, it seemed like a suitable gesture for such a happy occasion. Our other pig, Tanraki, would remain in school as part of the Agricultural Department's ongoing study.

On the Saturday morning of the wedding, several of the older boys from school appeared at our house to take Ezmeralda away. Not wanting to miss out on the preparations, I followed them as they walked to the lagoon side of Rongorongo.

It was yet another occasion when youngsters displayed the traditional skills they had inherited. I was fascinated as they carried out the slaughtering, pre-cooking preparation, the making of a traditional pit oven, the cooking and the eventual extraction of the pig from the pit. Like a collective machine, they confidently carried out these age-old tasks that had been successfully handed down to them. After two years, you would think that it was impossible to be impressed by what these young people could do within their atoll world. But it was not!

A few hours later, the wedding ceremony took place in the school church. Temonari was dressed in a white wedding dress complete with veil and long train; Betero wore a grey suit, white shirt and tie. In recent years more European attire had obviously been taken on board for such occasions and they wouldn't have looked out of place in Auckland or Vancouver.

After leaving the church, the happy couple meandered across Rongorongo followed by the entire school in a long procession. After several speeches inside the maneaba there was a feast of Gilbertese delicacies, including our pig. Naturally, the obligatory singing and dancing rounded off this marriage ceremony between these two fledgling Rongorongo teachers.

Such an occasion emphasised that for another married couple, Jackie and me, our days on Beru were rapidly coming to an end. It was time to prepare for our departure and consider our future, wherever it might take us.

With our two-year term complete, VSO would soon be providing flights for us to return back to the UK. Then what would we do? Where would we live? Would we go back to the Black Country in the English Midlands? With airmail letters between the Gilbert Islands and the UK sometimes taking six weeks, it hadn't been easy to apply for jobs. The postal service was somewhat unreliable and letters and parcels were occasionally lost. If there were any dried foods in a package, which our parents were in the habit of sending, invariably rats or mice consumed the contents along the way. However, our Yorkshire friends, Ruth and Alan, solved this problem when they successfully sent a rich fruit cake sealed in a tin. It was so yummy that the item disappeared in one sitting on our veranda as soon as it arrived!

Fortunately, I had been accepted on a part-time course at Cartrefle College in Wrexham in North Wales, where Jackie and I had initially trained to be teachers. This meant we had to find somewhere to work close to North Wales. After numerous letters asking for teaching jobs with different educational authorities nearby, we eventually received a reply from Wigan in the North of England:

If you both present yourselves at our Department Building, here in Wigan, we will try to put you on our supply teaching list.

As it was the only offer we'd had – even if it was only a possibility – that was where Jackie and I would be heading. It was a definite leap into the unknown but, we now had an aim: for us both to work in the north of England and for me to complete a part-time course in North Wales. We were happy with that.

There were a number of final tasks to complete before we left. We made sure our plans for our subjects were ready for others to continue with the work, and we checked the resources we had been using were organised. We talked through the teaching that had taken place, individual progress students had made and their next stages with the members of staff who were taking over our jobs.

Jackie and I were both reasonably satisfied with how the teaching programmes for English, social studies and our other curriculum areas had developed. However, there would always be room for improving the teaching at the school. Top of the list would be to have more resources and expertise.

However, after two years on Beru we were both fairly content with the work we had carried out. Like teachers the world over, we all think there is more we could have done; that is the nature of the work.

All we needed to do was to pack our few belongings into suitcases ready for our departure. We had brought just a few essential possessions when we arrived and didn't have much more to take back. Any extra items we had acquired during our two years we simply gave away.

The school caretaker, Kristian, took over our government pig and chickens and said our dog, Charlie, could live with him and his family. This pleased us because we had become quite attached to the unusual hound. I suppose we had indulged Charlie like most British do with their pets, so we hoped he would be okay when we finally left. We had to remember that he had been fine during the times we had been on Tarawa when Kristian had looked after him.

It was time to reflect on our time on Beru. As VSOs, how much had we given to the lives of these pupils compared to how much we, as two foreigners, had gained from our experiences on their island? Was this 'give and take' in balance, or was it more of a one-sided affair?

Hopefully during our two years we had increased the pupils' ability to use the English language, as well as introducing them to aspects of the world beyond the Gilbert Islands via their social studies. And, of course, by interacting with the pupils there may well have been other areas in which we had helped or influenced them.

The pupils had always been receptive to new learning and they had been great to work with. They were happy and contented students who respected their peers and those who helped them through their schooling. Unlike the UK, there were never any discipline problems in our entire two years!

We hoped that we had helped them pass exams that might lead to employment opportunities. Some may argue that would ultimately result in a 'brain drain' from the outer islands to Tarawa, the main island, or to somewhere abroad. That was always a possibility but, given the circumstances of these youngsters, who were we to say that would be wrong?

Losing traditional skills and diluting culture is undesirable, but if we were the pupils or their family members, wouldn't we wish for the very best life could offer in whatever way that might pan out? It is a difficult debate and one which continues as part of the developing world conundrum.

For Jackie and I, there was one striking aspect of living in a traditional island society. The islanders appeared to be far more in tune and connected with nature than more urban or so-called 'advanced' societies. The Gilbertese understood the lunar cycle, that governed the tide and the type and number of fish available to eat. Possessing such knowledge determined what fishing could take place and where. That understanding is crucial for survival on an island only two or three metres above the water line in the vast Pacific Ocean.

Surprisingly, the spathes of coconut trees, so important for karawe and copra production, also kept to a lunar cycle, so knowing the stage the moon was critical for success. Such an alliance with nature was central to the islanders' success and I believe it made both Jackie and I more aware of humankind's place within nature and endorsed our already 'green' leanings!

The two years in the islands had been a mixed experience: on the one hand a struggle, but on the other a privileged view into a different world. We knew that to succeed in living on this 'desert-island' would probably be the hardest challenge of our lives. Nothing in our futures could ever present such an intense test.

The daily routine of finding food, working at a school with such meagre resources, and the restraints of living on an atoll were not easy, but it had been a privilege to live in such a different culture and to witness how this traditional world functioned. We had challenged our familiar lifestyle and, as previous VSO recruits agreed, the experience had broadened our minds.

Dick Bird has written a history of VSO: *Never The Same Again*. I'm sure most of us would concur that it is a perfect title. As the days before departure ticked by, Jackie and I agreed we had probably changed forever as individuals!

We lay as usual in the night heat beneath our mosquito net, listening to the familiar sounds of waves on the nearby shore, the faint shuffle of geckos on the ceiling, the rats playfully scurrying around and the frustrated mosquitoes attempting to get through the tight mesh of our net, and reflected on what we would miss. The list had to include the flow of the laid-back island life and the natural beauty of the people, their sense of humour, their expressive smiles and their earthiness.

We would miss the relationships we had made with teachers, other school staff and, of course, the pupils. Yes, we would miss the students who made up the school.

We would miss the red, purple and orange of each dawn and dusk, and the crystal-clear night skies with their myriad of stars, nights with a full moon so bright we could read a book on the veranda. I would miss my karewe tree, and we would both miss the singing. Oh, that singing!

Before we knew it, we were attending our farewell feast in the school maneaba, where there were many kind words about our time at Hiram Bingham High School. It was a fitting conclusion – this was something at which the Gilbertese were particularly masterful. Such formalities were part of a great tradition stretching back hundreds of years.

The speeches filled us with warmth and sadness. We were presented with traditional handicrafts including beautifully woven baskets and woven mats, embroidered pillow cases and other skilfully produced sundries.

In return, we gave long and heartfelt speeches. Then it was time for our last feast in the Rongorongo maneaba and a few prayers and singing to carry us safely on our way.

We shook hands, we hugged, we said so many goodbyes, then we were whisked off to the airstrip on the backs of motorbikes, clinging to our cases and gifts.

As we left the school grounds on that dirt track for the very last time, our dog Charlie galloped alongside us. He had never behaved in such a way before – he was far too laid-back. As he ran along and barked his goodbyes, our already tearful eyes filled a little more.

The smiles of Rongorongo

Jackie dancing in the school maneaba during our last days on Beru

Our inter-island plane on Beru

Friendly faces

Chapter 15

Visiting High Islands on Our Way to Aoraki

We flew over atoll islands far below us: Tabiteuea, Nonouti and Abemama, circular green lines amid the vivid blue of the Pacific.

Jackie and I were trying to come to terms with what would be our last journey across these Gilbertese islands. We were leaving! Our minds were a jumble of events from the past few days, and we were beginning to feel excited about our long trip home and to fantasise about our new lives back in the UK. Our heads were everywhere!

Apparently our inter-island plane was in need of repair and should have been grounded. The Fijian pilot, Captain Tuisue, realising we were leaving, made sure we were collected from Beru. That was a very friendly gesture, though we did become aware of an unusual flapping of loose aluminium coming from a section of the fuselage! Any maintenance would have to wait until the following day.

Tuisue had an interesting hobby: collecting traditional hats made on different islands. We had once found him a Beru hat made out of pandanus, which was used by the fishermen on the island.

Some twenty or so years later, there was a very strange occurrence. At the time I was teaching in a primary school in Bolton in the North of England when a nine-year-old Fijian girl turned up. Her dad had just started a year-long course at the local university. She was totally at a loss in her new surroundings and obviously missing Fiji.

I tried to cheer her up. I showed her a book about planes, in which she had told me she had an interest. As we looked through the book together, I told her that my favourite airline in the whole world was Air Pacific. Seeing her eyes light up, I told her I had once known and flown with a Captain Tuisue. She stated,

'Captain Tuisue? He is my uncle!'

I was totally taken aback! Wanting to check this information, I pried a little more.

'Tell me, did your uncle have any hobbies? Did he have an interesting collection of anything?'

She immediately referred to his unusual hats. I was amazed and she enjoyed that link with home. Now that is what I consider to be an amazing coincidence!

As is often the way, she soon made friends and quickly settled down into her new surroundings.

After we landed at Bonriki Airport, we threw our things and ourselves into the back of a waiting pick-up. As on similar rides on Tarawa, the driver avoided a scattering of coconut tree fronds and potholes on the way to Bikenibeu, where we were staying overnight.

Not long after our arrival, we were standing in the same maneaba where we had made our first speech two years previously. Before us sat men and women associates of Hiram Bingham High School and the church.

Jackie and I offered the assembled group kind words but with more confidence than during our first encounter. We talked of the work we had undertaken, about how we would miss the school and the Gilbert Islands. In turn, we were presented with heartfelt thoughts together with more gifts. This gathering rekindled the emotion Jackie and I had experienced earlier that day on Beru.

The following day we boarded an Air Nauru jet at Tarawa and, after two years working as VSOs, we left the Gilbert Islands. So began our grand journey back to the UK.

We had decided we wouldn't make a rapid dash for home; instead we would take a more meandering route. We wanted to visit some of the other island nations and enjoy locations we might never get the chance to see again.

The social studies units we had been teaching had made us curious to see some of the 'high islands' of the Pacific; we wanted to see 'three-dimensional' islands that had inland areas, hills, rivers, farming, towns and traffic. We were going to investigate, and these islands would do for starters on our journey. We also intended visiting a few larger countries as well; we had planned quite a trip.

The bigger, more deluxe aircraft we were on reflected the wealth of the nation it represented. We had heard plenty about Nauru whilst we were in the Gilberts; it was a place many Gilbertese mentioned where relatives worked and a whole range of goods might be obtained.

Geologically, Nauru is different to the Gilbert Islands because it is a raised coral island possessing an interior plateau with a high point of 71m above sea level! Such elevation wasn't to be snorted at by those who had been on an island where the highest point was only two or three metres above the sea.

Interestingly, over thousands of years Nauru had been visited by a great number of migrating birds who, over time, had deposited enormous amounts of their droppings. This guano had gradually built up until it made a vast layer of phosphate. Since the early 1900s this mineral had been mined by Australia, New Zealand and Britain and used as fertiliser to improve agricultural yields. After achieving independence in 1968, the mining was taken over by the Nauruan government, which resulted in the Nauruans becoming exceedingly wealthy. By the mid-1970s, it was the second wealthiest country on the planet after Saudi Arabia!

Under a cloudless blue sky, we could see Nauru below us as our plane prepared to land. Just as our teaching resources had stated:

...an oval-shaped island, five kilometres by four kilometres with a 19-kilometre road around its perimeter. It is the smallest island nation in the world; the third smallest after the Vatican City and Monaco; and, the least visited country on the planet!

A pick-up provided by the church was there to meet us. As many Gilbert Islanders lived and worked on Nauru, a link was maintained with their church.

We were driven to our hotel where we planned to simply relax, have a meal, sleep in a plush bed and prepare for our onward flight the following day. No chance! Word was out that the two VSOs who had been teaching at Hiram Bingham High

School were on Nauru. Once again we were whisked off for a feast with the Gilbertese Protestant Church community, and once again we enjoyed Gilbertese fare.

We gave a speech about our work at the school and our feelings about leaving. We were certain that this would be the final time we would be required to produce a maneaba-style speech. After the more formal part of the evening, a few of those gathered asked about their young relatives at the school.

After a good night's sleep in that plush bed, we were invited on a drive around Nauru before our plane departed. Undoubtedly, this small nation possessed a great deal of wealth and we couldn't help comparing its obvious affluence to Beru.

The favoured transportation for most Nauruans appeared to be powerful motorbikes which roared on the tarmac perimeter road in both directions. Along this outer ring of the island, people lived in a variety of settlements and used fewer traditional materials for their housing.

We had learnt of Nauruan excesses, which included most food items having to be brought in from overseas. Consequently, the diet of the population had suffered, resulting in many people becoming overweight. Most Nauruans didn't work – they left that to foreigners, including a sizeable Gilbertese workforce.

Towards the centre of the island, there was evidence of the strip mining of phosphate; in places the land had an almost moonscape appearance, with protruding upward pinnacles mixed with stony sand. Great chunks of the interior had been eaten away and appeared lifeless.

At points along the coast, giant cantilever metal booms stretched out to sea. Each of these complicated arms had a long conveyor belt running along its length to carry the crushed phosphate into the bowels of ships. At the end of one such boom, a ship was gradually being filled up with the mineral; no doubt it would sail away when full to improve the fertility of some faraway soil.

This was a very different landscape compared to Beru, a massive quarry-like environment compared to our relatively untouched atoll. We had been given a glimpse of Nauru and had found it strangely fascinating, though it suffered from obvious exploitation and degradation.

We were travelling in a south-west direction towards Fiji, our next destination. This would be our second visit and we now knew a little more about this much larger Pacific Island nation.

Out of the 332 Fijian islands two have a sizeable area, Viti Levu and Vanua Levu, but only about half are actually inhabited. Arguably, the country has a greater profile than either the Gilbert Islands or Nauru; Fiji is the location people associate with images of Pacific islands!

It is renowned for its rugged landscapes, coconut-tree lined beaches and coral reefs: an archetypal tropical paradise. But when we delved a little deeper than mere 'holiday brochure' imagery, we found this Pacific island nation had a rich, complex and sometimes worrying back story.

Fijians are Melanesian, belonging to the indigenous peoples of the south-west Pacific region, as opposed to the Micronesian peoples to the north, which include the Gilbert islanders. Historically, Fijians practised a traditional subsistence life living off both the land and sea, and had a richly developed cultural identity. In 1874, the island nation became a colony of Britain, after which sugar plantations were eventually established across swathes of the land. The colonial leaders took it upon themselves to ship indentured labourers from India to Fiji to work in the sugar plantations.

Over time, these newcomers from India (or Indo-Fijians, as they became known) increased in number. In 1970 Fiji became an independent state with a population comprising almost equal numbers of Fijians and Indo-Fijians. Unfortunately this led to a degree of tension between the two groups which has occasionally resulted in fractious encounters.

Fiji has become a significant commercial, transport, tourist and educational centre within the Pacific region. Indeed, those social studies materials we used on Beru were written and produced at the University of the South Pacific (based in the capital, Suva), which is a hub for tertiary studies for huge numbers of Pacific island students.

Our New Zealand pilot friend, John, and his wife, Diana, had invited us to stay with them in Suva during the couple of days of this leg of our homeward journey.

The most outstanding experience was a trip through the centre of Suva. Jackie and I stared in bewilderment at the large city buildings, wide tarmac roads, pavements, traffic, crowds of people, range of shops and the general hustle and bustle. Police wore white lavalava (called '*sulu*') as part of their uniforms and stood in key positions directing traffic.

There was so much going on that we were awestruck by what we saw, heard and smelled; it was quite an encounter for the senses. But more shocks were about to occur as we caught our next flight straight into a New Zealand winter!

After meeting us at the airport, John's dad drove us to a motel in the suburbs of Auckland. As we sat in the back of the car, it was obvious that we were now in an even bigger urban centre than the one we had just left in Fiji.

We looked around us as we travelled across the city and our tropically attuned bodies instantly noticed the drop in temperature. Having lived on Beru for two years, we were experiencing both a culture and climate shock.

Once inside the motel, and with the heating fully turned up, we continued to feel the chill creeping in from the outside. Thankfully my mum had shipped out a couple of jumpers and we had also found some trousers, shoes and socks in Suva. But, we were still cold – no, we were freezing!

We managed to survive the night, cuddled up in bed and still wearing most of our clothes. After breakfast we had a few hours to spare so, like a demented lemming, I prepared to go out for a run. Yes, a run! Over the past two years I had kept fit by going for a run every other day and I prided myself on having missed only a few of these, which I considered to be essential work-outs during our time in the Gilbert Islands. I aimed to continue exercising all the way back to the UK, no matter where we were.

'*What are you doing?*' Jackie enquired.

'*I'm going out for a run.*'

'*Are you crazy? Have you looked out of the window? It's cold out there!*'

She spoke as though we had entered some kind of alien land; her words had a definite sci-fi ring to them. After our years together, I could now recognise her look of despair at my somewhat strange behaviour.

Shorts and T-shirt on. Trainers on. After two years running on a tropical island, my footwear was looking decidedly worn out; the salty atmosphere had attacked my shoes like all of our garments.

I opened the door, stepped out and took a breath. Surely the overnight temperature must have fallen close to zero? Every breath was visible as it billowed from my mouth, the cold air pierced my lungs and it hurt to breathe. I coughed and started to shiver, then started to run and take in ever deeper breaths. It was extraordinarily painful.

One of the reasons for running is to experience the endorphin rush – that feel-good factor – but this particular run was sheer torture and I literally staggered through the motions.

I was only out for about twenty minutes. After I had warmed up a little and donned most of my clothes, we left the motel. Before we arrived at the bus station, we bought a couple of thick, checked, woollen jackets and pulled them over our heads; we looked like lumberjacks.

We bought tickets to the city of Rotorua, around three hours away to the southeast of Auckland. Why go to Rotorua? Well, for two reasons really. The first was to continue our investigation of the Pacific region and its people. The indigenous people of New Zealand, the Māoris, have a strong historical link to Rotorua; there were locations in and around the city that we wanted to visit to gain a little insight into the Māori culture.

These Polynesian people are found right across the Pacific, including Tonga, Samoa, Tuvalu, northwards to Hawaii and eastwards to Tahiti and Easter Island. Sometime around 1200–1300, a number of Polynesians travelled in large canoes to what is now New Zealand, and over the years Māori culture gradually evolved.

The other reason for our visit was that the Rotorua area is famous for its geothermal activity; as a geological nerd, it was an opportunity for me to see some of the volcanic features I'd heard about when I was studying the subject.

I remembered that New Zealand is at one end of the Ring of Fire, a 40,000-kms curve of volcanic and earthquake activity that circles the Pacific Ocean from where we were, along Eastern Asia then down the western side of North and South America.

As we journeyed along the streets of Rotorua, we started to smell that 'rotten egg' odour the city is famous for. Due to the continuous emission of hydrogen sulphide it is always in the air; indeed, Rotorua has gained the nickname 'Sulphur City'.

Even though it was winter in New Zealand, finding somewhere to stay wasn't a problem. After being dropped off at the bus station, we secured a room in the first hotel we came to. Wandering through the streets, we found a place to eat and somewhere with tourist information. We booked a bus tour for the next day that would take us to the locations we wanted to visit.

Walking back to our hotel and in our room, there was that constant pong of sulphur. The lady running the establishment commented,

'Ah, you get used to it after a while. I never notice it.'

But as we went to sleep, the smell of rotten eggs just wouldn't go away.

The next day we found the single-decker bus standing ready to welcome tourists and clambered aboard. When we were seated, the driver turned around and asked us our names. He started the engine, adjusted the onboard microphone and sound system – and as he drove off, we saw we were the only tourists on the bus!

He spoke into his mike,

'Welcome aboard, Jackie and Roger. My name is George and today I will be taking you around a variety of sites of interest in Rotorua.'

George proceeded to give the history of the Rotorua region, its geothermal activity and how the area had first been inhabited by various Māori groups, interjecting his commentary with 'Jackie' and 'Roger' and providing us with a very personalised guided tour. It was midwinter and few tourists were around but I did wonder: if the bus had been packed, would he have referred to all forty passengers by name?

At the Māori Centre we were fascinated with the artwork being created by hugely talented artists and crafts people. There were examples of wood carvings, weaving, paintings and tattooing. Men and women were working away at their creations as we looked at a host of items on display. There was a commonality across the art forms, with distinctive bold designs, patterns and colour. Both of us were very impressed.

'Now, Jackie and Roger, at our next stop you can witness geothermal activity. Make sure that you see...' and George reeled off a list of geological features to look out for.

We were not disappointed. These were features of igneous geology I had been hearing about for years. Since leaving school, my interest had continued; I had a collection of geological samples back in the UK. And here I was, about to see some of these physical igneous features for real.

We were at Whakarewarewa geothermal area, a location Māoris had lived in since the early 1300s. Geothermal action galore: hot bubbling mud pools; steaming vents; sinter terraces, and layers of sulphur deposits from the mineral-rich waters gushing upwards.

The highlight of the walk was, of course, a couple of spurting geysers that were shooting many metres into the air! These were the Mahanga and the Waikorohiki geysers; they were so impressive that Jackie and I simply stopped and stared. As a collector of geological specimens, I very naughtily couldn't resist acquiring a small sample of sulphur from the edge of one of these gaseous outbursts from inside the earth!

'I hope you enjoyed the geothermal activity, Jackie and Roger. At our next stop you will be able to see the New Zealand national bird, the kiwi!'

The nocturnal kiwi birds were in specially constructed enclosures in semi-darkness. These creatures had become one of the key symbols of the nation. It is little wonder they earned such an accolade because they have a long list of unique features. About the size of a chicken, they have small wings and are flightless; their feathers are similar to fur; they have an acute sense of smell with nostrils at the end of their beaks, and they have whiskers! Kiwis feature extensively throughout Māori culture.

Unfortunately their numbers were on the decline. Jackie and I desperately tried to get a glimpse of these shy birds in their almost lightless pens and eventually we succeeded when a couple of them appeared.

George returned us to our starting point in Rotorua.

'Well, Jackie and Roger, I hoped you enjoyed your tour of Rotorua. I wish you well and hope to see you again some time.'

With that, we left our bus and went back to our hotel.

Continuing our investigation into the ways of the Pacific, in the evening we went along to a Māori concert in a hall near where we were staying. The performance included singing and dancing, with all those taking part of Māori descent and wearing traditional costumes. It was impressive, particularly the use of facial expressions, chanting, arm movements, distinctive bulging eyes and outstretched tongues. There were vigorous movements – stomping of feet, slapping of thighs and chest – and shouting and grunting.

We couldn't help comparing it to Gilbertese singing and dancing. The rhythms were similarly exact and heartfelt but the Māori facial movements were very exaggerated and occasionally aggressive, whereas with Gilbertese performances they are not.

Over the years, since Europeans took over their land, Māori culture must have been severely modified. As more waves of settlers from the other side of the world arrived in New Zealand, Māori culture was suppressed, their way of life changed and their ancestral lands taken. Such turmoil led to a series of wars between the indigenous Māori and the European settlers, which only came to a halt in 1872. Even though the fighting had stopped about a hundred years earlier, there still existed a degree of disquiet at the injustices the Māori people had endured.

After our visits to Nauru and Fiji, this was yet another Pacific country that had experienced unfortunate colonial encounters. As Jackie and I sat watching the concert, a degree of circumspection filled our mood. We were impressed with the Māori performance and the passion of those taking part, but we were suddenly filled with pleasure that we had been in the Gilbert Islands where there didn't appear to be such a loss of culture and a disintegration of the traditional way of life. We had been privileged to see a Pacific culture that was alive and vibrant on our outer island!

The following day we travelled further down the North Island of New Zealand on a Mount Cook coach to the capital city, Wellington, in the south of the island. Along the way, the coach pulled off the main road to allow passengers a break.

As we looked beyond the roadside fence, we saw a geothermal power station spread out before us. Huge silver pipes crossed the nearby fields and connected with many more pipes from a different direction. Great gushes of steam were rising into the air. I noticed bore-hole samples scattered on the ground: cylindrically cut samples of breccia rock, some five centimetres in diameter. No doubt, these had been part of the drilling process linked to the geothermal extraction. This was another opportunity to add a rock sample to my collection.

It was impressive how New Zealand was tapping into such energy. Lying on the Ring of Fire has certain disadvantages in that the country is prone to earthquakes and volcanic activity, but there are also advantages in having a geothermal energy source.

We stayed for one night in Wellington before crossing the Cook Strait to the South Island. From the port of Picton, we travelled on another Mount Cook coach to Christchurch. We stayed for one night in the South Island's biggest city before moving on again, this time inland.

Whilst cutting karewe on my coconut tree on Beru, I had occasionally looked in a southerly direction. As a lover of mountains, I would sometimes mutter, *'More than 5,000kms in that direction are the Southern Alps. Mountains, snow and glaciers!'*

I would take a moment to daydream as I swayed in my coconut tree. It was 'mountain meditation!' Boarding another coach out of Christchurch, we were about to realise that dream: we were off to see Mount Cook or 'Aoraki' as the Māori call it.

As the coach trundled along, the driver told us that the flat terrain we were crossing was called the Mackenzie Basin, named after James Mackenzie. During the 1850s, this settler from Scotland was an infamous sheep rustler who kept his stolen stock in the region. It was an interesting tale of how New Zealand was settled by many Europeans who sought to make a living by farming this land.

We drove through hills which gradually became mountains; we had arrived in the Southern Alps, with their snow-capped summits and glaciers. Daydream no more – we were in the mountains!

The bus dropped us off at Mount Cook village where we soon located the lodge we would stay in for three nights. These were bases where people could explore the mountains and carry out a range of activities. There were plenty of walks and climbs to enjoy but many of the excursions would be serious undertakings, even for those with the necessary mountain knowledge and skills. Front and centre, looking down the Hooker Valley, stood Aoraki, a classically formed, pointed summit standing 3724 metres high!

The Māori believe Aoraki is a sacred place. Legend tells of a man named Aoraki and his three brothers who were out in their canoe. They were the sons of Rakinui, the Sky Father, and were on a voyage around Papatuanuka, the Earth Mother.

On their journey across the ocean, the vessel came to grief on a reef. The travellers were stranded and climbed on top of their upturned canoe. In a cold southerly wind blowing straight from Antarctica, they were all frozen and eventually turned to stone. The legend says that the canoe became Te Waka a Aoraki, otherwise known as the South Island of New Zealand. Aoraki, being the tallest of the travellers, became the highest peak of the island. His brothers and the remaining crew members became the other summits of the Southern Alps.

There appeared to be few people in this beautiful mountainous hub. Inside the region's information centre, I was amazed to find that only a couple of groups were out on winter expeditions! For the next two days, Jackie and I aimed to do a little straightforward mountain walking, something we hadn't done for some time. My good wife insisted I disappeared on my own the next day *'to get it out of your system!'*

I hired a pair of hiking boots but needed an ice-axe so I could walk along the edge of the Hooker Glacier. Luckily, one of the kitchen workers in the basement of the nearby Hermitage Hotel lent me one for a couple of days.

I set off along the flat valley floor and eventually reached the Hooker Glacier where I continued on a moraine path. It was just incredible! Absolute amazing! Clear mountain air, stark winter vegetation below, exposed rock, masses of ice and snow above – all under a cloudless sky!

The next day Jackie and I walked to the Mueller Glacier where we played in the snow and soaked up the endless views. Such superb mountain magic! But all too soon we were back on a coach again, wending our way back to Auckland.

The cantilever on Nauru ready to empty phosphate into a ship

The island nation of Nauru with its heavily mined interior

The Southern Alps of New Zealand with Aoraki in the distance

The sulphur emissions of Rotorua in New Zealand

Chapter 16

Visiting More High Islands on Our Way to Wigan

Our next leg of our Pacific journey took us 1800kms north east of New Zealand to the kingdom of Tonga, another Polynesian island nation. Jackie and I were keen to look at yet another high island location we had referred to during our lessons.

For a number of centuries Tonga was a dominant force across a huge area of the Pacific, from the Solomon Islands in the west, through Niue, Fiji, Samoa, to eastern Polynesia. It was known as the 'Tu'i Tonga Empire', which reached its peak between 1200 and 1500.

During this period there was an exchange of ideas and resources between these different islands. Double canoes, some carrying as many as a hundred people, journeyed huge distances to maintain this empire. The navigational and ocean-going sailing skills must have been exceedingly well-developed to have made possible such long trips across the Pacific Ocean.

Eventually, however, the dominance of Tonga waned. All through Tongan history there have been monarchs – both kings and queens – who have cemented the society together. Unlike other Pacific Islands, Tonga has continued as the only independent monarchy in the Pacific region.

In 1900 Tonga signed a Treaty of Friendship with Britain and voluntarily became a British Protectorate, but it was never formally colonised. In 1970 it achieved full sovereignty and independence.

Tonga consists of 169 islands, 36 of which are inhabited, and stretches some 800kms from north to south across the South Pacific. Many of the islands are very small and remote; Tongatapu is the biggest island in the far south of the group. These islands are on the Ring of Fire, close to tectonic plates, and are occasionally subjected to earthquake and volcanic activity.

The region's rich volcanic soil produces coconuts, vanilla beans, bananas and squash. Fishing, together with some tourism, also provide incomes for the Tongan people.

From the airport on Tongatapu we travelled to the capital, Nuku'alofa. This was also a more developed island than Beru, where we had been living. There were many cars, buses, shops, people and buildings.

Acquaintances had given us the name of a hotel where we could enjoy some good Tongan hospitality. We quickly unpacked and went off to explore the city. The following day we visited the Saturday market, hoping to buy a Tongan *tapa* cloth which, we had been told, were of the highest quality. Tapa cloth art is a distinctly Pacific Island creation and a number of islands produce fine examples. Indeed, we had already bought a circular tapa cloth in Fiji when we were passing through.

The cloth is produced by stripping lengths of inner bark from paper mulberry trees and leaving it to dry in the sun. These sections are spread on the floor and beaten with a special wooden hammer to make them thinner, then other lengths are added and beaten together to make a larger cloth. The final stage is to paint the cloth using age-old traditional designs.

The market was in full swing when we arrived, with hustle and bustle from the locals purchasing fruit, vegetables, other food and household items. There was an area selling handicrafts, amongst which were tapa cloths.

We selected a rather large two- by three-metre cloth with a golden-brown background on which there were five pictures including garlands, crowns, stars and birds. We assumed the crowns referred to the Tongan king, King Taufa'ahau Tupou IV. It was a splendid piece of art and we looked forward to hanging it with our Fijian tapa cloth back in the UK.

The following day was Sunday. We travelled back to the airport and flew to another Saturday market after crossing the International Dateline! Remembering my geography, I visualised the world being divided into different time zones like segments of an orange. As a general rule when travelling eastwards, one hour is gained for every fifteen degrees of longitude. However, there will be a line on that global journey where the end of one day will meet the beginning of the next: the International

Dateline. When a person crosses it travelling from west to east, an entire twenty-four hours will gain a day.

Illustrating this, flying from Tonga to our next destination, Western Samoa, meant taking off on Sunday and landing on Saturday. Even though the flight took just under two hours, we went back to the day before!

For a geography enthusiast, the experience was quite amazing; I was in nerd paradise! Taking off from Tongatapu Island in Tonga on Sunday, flying some 900kms, crossing the International Dateline and then landing on Upolu Island in Western Samoa on Saturday. Superb!

It must be pointed out that this was the case in 1978 when we were travelling. At that time, the International Dateline was drawn between Tonga and Western Samoa. In 2011 the International Dateline was redrawn further to the east between Western Samoa and American Samoa.

After settling into a small hotel, we went out to explore Apia, the capital of Western Samoa. (In 1978, the island nation was called Western Samoa and didn't change its name to Samoa until 1997.)

We refrained from purchasing another tapa cloth, although those on display were extremely good. The Saturday market was full of excitement like the one we had visited the previous day. Apia appeared to have similar urbanisation, many vehicles, people, large buildings and a variety of goods in the stores.

Reflecting yet again on our social studies work at Rongorongo, we could see why some of the units of work suited the more developed Pacific islands compared with life on outer-island atolls.

As we wandered around, we spotted a traditional oval-shaped Samoan *fale*. These are open-sided, thatched-roofed meeting houses similar to Gilbertese maneabas, where important ceremonies, meetings and events take place.

The Polynesian nation of Western Samoa consists of two main islands: Savai'i, the bigger of the two, and Upolu, where the capital Apia is located. These two islands make up 99% of the land mass with several much smaller islands making up the rest.

Western Samoa is also volcanic in origin; on our walk near the coast in Apia, I became very excited when I spotted some amazing volcanic rock samples. Jackie's face is always a picture of disbelief on these occasions.

All around us the most perfect pahoehoe lava was scattered on the ground. This black rock was sharp and looked as though it had been subjected to folding, like slabs of black pastry. It was easy to imagine how such rock had once flowed out of a volcano; you could see the folds as it had slowly moved along before finally coming to a halt. When it was on the move, the lava would have been red but when it eventually stopped it cooled and turned black. Another chance to add to the geological collection.

Samoa, like other Polynesian islands, had evolved over the centuries through inter-island travel, including on one occasion, being part of that Tongan Empire. More recently, between 1900 and 1914, Samoa was taken over by the German Empire. The colonisers developed copra, cocoa, banana and rubber plantations on the islands. However, from 1914, the New Zealand government was in charge and it became the Western Samoa Trust Territory.

Throughout its New Zealand tenure, a non-violent resistance movement steadily gained in popularity throughout Western Samoa. Over the years, the Mau Movement, as this anti-colonial group was known, resented being governed by New Zealand which they blamed for a range of problems. The colonisers, in an attempt to control the islanders, restricted the locals' movements and took away the powers of traditional Samoan leaders, all part of a deliberate policy of oppression and restraint.

In addition, around a quarter of the population died after the Spanish flu pandemic spread across Western Samoa. The colonial government of New Zealand was blamed for the way it handled the pandemic.

Some of the Mau ringleaders were exiled and there were many accounts of violence by the colonial police towards the islanders. The worst of these occurred in 1927, when eleven Mau protesters were killed and sixty were injured when the colonial police opened fire during a peaceful protest.

Eventually Western Samoa gained its independence in 1962, the first small island state in the Pacific to do so.

For Jackie and me, once again it was time to move on. After a flight lasting just over half an hour, we were taxiing to a standstill on the runway of Pago Pago Airport on the island of Tutuila in American Samoa.

Making our way through the arrivals department, it was obvious that we had entered an entirely different Pacific island. We immediately detected far more wealth and development; this was American Samoa, a territory of the United States and the most southerly of all its geographical possessions.

Neither Jackie nor I had ever visited America, but it felt as though we had just arrived there. As we made our way to the capital, Pago Pago and found somewhere to stay, the whole flavour of what was around us said 'America'. There had obviously been a lot of development creating buildings, roads, vehicles, shops full of US goods in an altogether American atmosphere.

After developing as a single Samoan nation during its early history, in 1899 the Samoan islands were divided up by the colonial powers. The United States took control of the eastern islands and a navy station was built in the natural harbour of Pago Pago. This partitioning of Samoa continued even when New Zealand took over German-controlled Western Samoa at the end of World War One.

When the Spanish flu pandemic threatened American Samoa, the commander of the Pago Pago naval base imposed a strict blockade around the islands. Fortunately it kept the virus out and, as a result, there were no Spanish flu deaths in American Samoa.

The Mau resistance movement did not develop to the same extent in American Samoa as it had done in Western Samoa. It has been suggested that the way the pandemic was handled in both places had a bearing on the unrest in Western Samoa.

During World War Two, huge numbers of US military personnel were stationed in Pago Pago and this led to an increase in the United States' cultural influence.

Many islanders joined the US military and some moved to areas of the United States. When Western Samoa became independent in 1962, the five volcanic islands and two atolls of American Samoa were quite content to remain as a territory of the United States.

When Jackie and I visited in 1978, we walked to the US naval base and other shipping-related buildings in Pago Pago. Around the harbour was a rugged, forested, volcanic landscape rising to jagged peaks.

The highlight of our short stay was a cable-car ride up to Mount Alava, 491m above Pago Pago. When it was constructed in 1965 it was one of the world's longest single-track cable-car routes. It was an amazing feat of human construction, with carefully positioned metal towers, thick cables, cable cars, power sources and delicate gravity-defying engineering.

It was the first cable-car ride Jackie and I had taken, although there would be many more in the future. Once again, it was not what someone would expect to find on a Pacific island! But what a breath-taking vista at the top, with the natural harbour of Pago Pago and the surrounding volcanic landscape spread out below. American Samoa was definitely a very different island location.

Next we flew to the last set of Pacific islands that we had planned to visit. We travelled more than 4,000kms in a north-easterly direction to the most northerly part of Polynesia: the islands of Hawaii.

As we descended out of the sky, beneath us lay the island of O'ahu. We landed at the airport and made our way to Honolulu, the capital city. This was a whole different level of development and sophistication. We had been amazed at what we had seen in Pago Pago, but for a couple of people who had been in a very basic island environment for two years, the next couple of days were quite mind blowing!

We went to the famous Waikiki beach area of Honolulu and found a place to stay. Venturing outside the hotel, we struggled to comprehend what we could see around us.

Along the extensive beach front were masses of hotels, many of them high-rise. These huge buildings towered unnaturally over the flat blue of the ocean. A few brave trees were desperately clinging on, making a last stand against a backdrop of encroaching concrete.

It was extremely urbanised – and it was unsettling. There were numerous beachside cafes and bars, tourists on loungers soaking up the sun, others swimming or playing in the sea and yet more ambling along in this world-renowned holiday hotspot. Our

Rongorongo senses were stunned! Shocked! How could a Polynesian island have developed into this? What was its story?

These 137 volcanic islands are situated in an archipelago spread over 2,400kms across a section of the northern half of the Pacific Ocean. Like other islands, the first people to visit came from far away as they explored in ocean-going canoes. Many believe that the first inhabitants travelled from the Polynesian islands of Marquesas and Tahiti and settled in Hawaii around a thousand years ago.

In these large, fertile tropical islands, different chiefdoms eventually evolved and flourished. Occasionally battles broke out between the different groups in order to settle a variety of disputes, but the inter-chiefdom fighting eventually ceased in 1795 when the various clans across the islands were unified under one leader, King Kamehameha I.

In 1843 Hawaii was recognised as an independent nation by a proclamation made by both Britain and France. In time there followed a host of European and American explorers, traders and whalers to the islands, together with many missionaries wanting to convert the inhabitants to Christianity. Unfortunately, these visitors brought diseases such as measles, influenza and smallpox. It has been estimated that half of the indigenous population was killed during this period.

In time, American and European entrepreneurs developed plantations throughout Hawaii growing sugar, coffee and pineapples among other crops, destined for locations abroad.

In 1893 a coup d'état took place when Western businessmen overthrew Queen Lili'uokaluni, the monarch at the time. This controversial act of disposing of the legitimate monarch led to Hawaii becoming a territory of the United States in 1898. What followed was greater commercial development for the islands, the construction of a large US naval base at Pearl Harbor and an influx of more foreigners, including Filipinos, Japanese, Koreans and Puerto Ricans migrating for work, many to the plantations.

The Japanese attacked the military facilities at Pearl Harbor in 1941, which led to the United States entering the Second World War. Finally, in 1959 Hawaii transitioned from territory to state and became the fiftieth state of the USA. The islands have continued to modernise and grow in prosperity as well as becoming a major tourist destination.

In need of some exercise, I decided to go for a run. Not far from our hotel I spotted a perfect location: a long, straight, pedestrianised pathway adjacent to some water where several other runners were already out.

I joined them. It was pleasant to run with other people with a similar mindset. Okay, Honolulu had jolted us into a more developed world, which psychologically we weren't prepared for, but, at least there was an acceptable area for a run! It was good to blend in with other runners and not be a strange, conspicuous object to be stared at.

I was impressed with this extensive area in which to exercise: reach the end, turn around and run back, repeat.

In the evening we ate at a beachside cafe and sampled some fast food. As we ate, we watched the antics on the beach and in the water. We were 'people watching' and were mesmerised!

The following day we thought we would see as much of O'ahu Island as possible during this fleeting visit. We caught a bus that took us around most of the island. Wanting to simply take in the scenery, Jackie and I stayed on the bus but it turned out to be quite an exhausting experience. All our Pacific travelling crossing numerous time zones resulted in us being lulled into a doze once we were gently travelling in a rocking bus. We were babes in a pram!

I forced myself to stay awake, realising this would probably be the only time I would visit O'ahu. The geographical nerd within was alive and kicking; there were simply too many features to look at. Jackie, on the other hand, fell asleep. If there was anything of real interest to view, I could wake her up.

The bus trip took many hours. It started with a view of the huge military facilities at Pearl Harbor, then many kilometres of fascinating volcanic features interspersed with beaches with yet more people frolicking on the sand and in the sea.

What really stood out were huge areas of pineapples growing as far as the eyes could see. Jackie awoke for this particular sight and we both gasped in amazement. Such sights just about fought off my fatigue and stopped me joining Jackie in a snooze.

After our bus trip and some reflection, we agreed that we had been disappointed with Hawaii. Like many before us, we had been fed an image of these islands as a Pacific paradise but they didn't come anywhere close, not after our visits to the other Pacific islands and our very own island of Beru! Had we been spoilt by living there? Hawaii had fallen short!

Others who visit Hawaii might well think differently. It is one of the intriguing aspects of travel: an opinion of a location depends very much upon our expectations and previous experiences.

It was time to leave; we had come to the end of our journey across the Pacific islands. We were pleased we had spent time visiting other island locations within this great ocean; we had learned a lot, even if we had only glimpsed them fleetingly.

It is said that travel broadens the mind and offers new ways of living and thinking. Our Pacific adventure had definitely succeeded in that.

We were now starting our North American leg of our homeward journey. Part of our grand plan was to look at the United States and make a brief visit to Canada.

We flew to San Francisco on the west coast and found a small hotel. Visiting Hawaii should have helped us adjust to this most famed of Californian locations, but it came as a further shock.

From our hotel, we wandered around the city. We caught one of the iconic trams or cable-cars; this legendary form of San Francisco transport is famed for its journeys up and down the city's hills.

Eventually we arrived at Fisherman's Wharf where we looked at the boats in the harbour and viewed distant Alcatraz Island. The area was full of tourists; obviously it was very much a place to visit in the city.

We caught a cab to return to our hotel and the driver took us through the downtown area of San Francisco. Jackie and I were fascinated to see some of the 'anti-earthquake' architecture the friendly cabby pointed out.

Since the massive earthquake of 1906, when more than 3000 people died, the city has attempted to minimise the risk of collapsing buildings with innovative designs. It wasn't only the earthquake that caused problems but also the devastating fires that followed. After the catastrophe, three-quarters of San Francisco was destroyed. It was a reminder that the Pacific Ring of Fire also runs down the length of both North and South America.

The San Andreas Fault is a geological fault line on the edge of a tectonic plate that follows the line of the Ring of Fire. It was movement along the San Andreas that caused the massive 1906 earthquake.

Later in the day I ventured out for another run. I must admit I felt distinctively uncomfortable as I ran around the highly urbanised but rather rundown area of the city. It was the unsettling looks from people just standing around and staring that I didn't enjoy. It was also an effort to run among volumes of traffic.

As we watched local television in the evening, there was a disturbing report about somebody being shot inside a tram travelling near Fisherman's Wharf. It was close to the time when we were there. Another eye-popping moment!

On the way to the airport the next day, our taxi driver drove us over the Golden Gate Bridge, an iconic sight we wished to see. The notorious fog hung across the bridge as we crossed, which brought to a close our brief stay in San Francisco.

Our desire to get the most out of our return trip to the UK had led to us to fly north to Canada for a couple of nights. From Vancouver airport we travelled to the centre of the city and found a room in a high-rise hotel.

Out of the window, around fifteen floors up in the sky, we could see a fair distance including a substantial marshalling yard. Long freight trains were loading up with logs ready to be hauled eastwards. It was a fascinating sight: diminutive trains far below, loading machines, people working, long trains slowly starting their journey and some arriving. We were agog. You could tell that we had experienced a sheltered couple of years!

At this point in our travels, Jackie and I lost a day. Once more the crossing of time zones, together with a general journeying fatigue, resulted in us spending most of the next day catching up on sleep.

The following morning we took a coach ride across the city through the plush houses of an area named 'British Properties'. We ended up at Grouse Mountain, a location for downhill skiing in winter and hiking during the summer.

Jackie and I found a marked hiking trail among the trees, over wooden suspension bridges and with Canadian mountain views. It was great to be amongst such immense conifers, a tonic after too much urbanisation, and a pleasure to be surrounded by nature and breathing in fresh air.

After flying for hours across the flat agricultural Midwest of the United States, we landed at O'Hare Airport in Chicago. For our final stop in North America, Alice, Jim and family had kindly invited us to stay with them for a few days. After being on Beru, this family had moved back to their home in America and wanted to show us the sights, sounds and life of the country.

The city was an immense, overwhelming place: big buildings, big cars, great numbers of people in a big urban environment. The family had a large house and we stayed in their basement, which had a bed surrounded by utility items, old toys, bikes, boxes, workbenches and tools. There were so many gadgets, more than we had seen in a long time. For us simple 'island folk', just turning an electric switch on and off was mind blowing enough!

It was school holiday time, so Jim wasn't teaching and the three children weren't at school. They had time on their hands to show us a little of what America was all about. They were extremely hospitable and generous with their time, as were their friends and family, all of whom were very down to earth.

One day we travelled into the centre of Chicago and caught a fast elevator to the top of Sear's Tower. At the time of our visit in 1978, this was the tallest building on the planet. Standing 442m above the city at the top of this 110-storey building, it was possible to look out and see four different US states on a clear day. From a window at the top we looked at vast numbers of tall buildings, a veritable skyscraper forest. Unfortunately, it was rather a smoggy day and we could only just see the ground far away below us.

With so many automobiles, it was no surprise that Chicago suffered from smog. We also noticed that the tower appeared to be swaying very gently! The ability to move in windy conditions is a design factor, with an average of a 15cms swing that could rise to 91cms in the windiest of conditions! We didn't ask what would happen if the wind took the sway-ability beyond its limit!

We learned that Chicago is nicknamed 'Windy City' because of the constant winds blowing across Lake Michigan. However, others say that the nickname came about due to the 'full of hot air' politicians who resided in the city in 1893 when Chicago competed with New York to hold an exposition. The editor of a New York newspaper at the time described Chicago as the Windy City because of its 'gas-bag city leaders!'

On another day, Alice took Jackie to a 'drive-thru' bank where her much bigger United Kingdom passport (compared with the US equivalent) got stuck in a tube during the transaction. After the problem was solved, they went to a movie. My wife was so impressed with *'the large buckets of Coca-Cola people were drinking'*.

Meanwhile, Jim decided to take me to a baseball game. According to him, this was essential fare for somebody who wanted to understand America. To get a real taste of the atmosphere, we sat in the 'bleachers' on the cheap bench seats in the zone for the everyday folk. In Chicago, those who sit in the bleachers are referred to as 'bleacher bums', and this was evidently the 'holy of holies' for baseball game enthusiasts.

As a person who hates all ball games including, cricket, football etc, etc, it seemed that the experience would be wasted on me. The most incredible part of the event was watching the mass of bodies at the stadium, thousands and thousands on all four sides above a green playing field below.

As far as the baseball went, there appeared to be a lot standing around by the players, with a bit of ball hitting, some catching, throwing, running, then back to standing. The noise at the height of the game was incredible! I spent practically the entire game watching the crowd cheer, boo, shout, eat, drink and hurl abuse.

Jim kindly tried to explain the finer points of baseball but they were lost on me. At the end, as the spectators filed out, we stayed behind for a while. I was amazed by the amount of litter left on the ground and on the benches: paper, Coke buckets, food, half-eaten burgers, drink canisters, wrappers, French fries, bits of hot dog ... it was just one mass of refuse. Such waste! I imagined the amount of rubbish left behind after this one game would probably equate to that of an entire year in the Gilbert Islands!

Our visit to our Chicago family soon came to an end and it was time to bid these kind, generous folk goodbye. Jackie and I had both experienced an overpowering few days as we were exposed to life in the United States; time now for our final flight and our return to the UK.

We landed at Heathrow Airport in London and were greeted by Jackie's mum and dad who had driven from South Wales. Once we had piled our belongings into their car, we travelled to Oxford to my parents' house for a reunion with two sets of parents and my aunt who lived with my mum and dad.

Jackie and I had many tales to tell about our life on Beru and our long trip back to the UK. They, in return, told us their news and it was an opportunity to reconnect.

One thing they commented on was that we had both developed some unusual habits! The most noticeable was when wanting to say 'yes' we simply raised our eyebrows. We also pointed with our noses and, when asked the time, pointed to where the sun should be. Our families found this somewhat amusing, to say the least.

'Would you like a drink?' Our eyebrows would rise and fall.

'Where did you put your bag?' With our noses, we would point to the chair where the item lay.

'What was the hottest time of the day in Beru?' Our fingers would point directly upwards.

We hadn't noticed them before, but these were some of the Gilbertese traits we had inherited. Now we were back in the UK, maybe a few communication adjustments were in order. And, although we openly admit to not having learnt much of the Gilbertese language, we did appear to be using a number of island words during these days of reunion. Evidently certain utterances had become ingrained: *e eng* (yes), *tiaki* (no), *ko rab'a* (thank you), *mauri* (hello), amongst others. We felt a certain degree of pride that a part of the islands had remained with us!

For the final part of our travels, we caught a train north to Wigan in Lancashire. It was a place neither of us had been to before or had any connection with – rather like going to Beru!

Once there, we hoped to find somewhere to live and work. We were planning to visit the Education Office in the town and take along our airmail letter with those words:

If you both present yourselves at our department building, here in Wigan, we will try to put you on our supply teaching list.

It was a long shot, which we hoped would result in us both finding teaching jobs.

As the train came to a halt at Wigan North Western Station, we dragged out our luggage and, like many a migrant to a new place, looked for the nearest place to stay.

It has been said that people in a new location will settle as far as they can physically haul their bags. Evidently, this was particularly true about the Irish, Scottish and others who moved to urban areas during the industrial revolution, and so it was for us.

Looking up and down the road, we spotted *The Swan and Railway Hotel*, less than a hundred metres away. We carried our belongings into the hotel and booked a room. Inside, we had a hot drink, clinked our cups, made a toast to the Gilbert Islands and gave each other a smile. We had completed the circle and were ready to start the next chapter of our lives.

High views of Pango Pango in American Samoa

The Saturday market in Nuku'alofa in Tonga

Part Two

Since we left, the islands have undergone changes and are now known as the Republic of Kiribati. This new nation, with its four scattered regions across the Pacific Ocean, has some unique geography and some historical tales to tell; however, of greatest concern is the threat of steadily rising sea levels. What will the future of these low-lying islands be?

Chapter 17

Kiribati

After returning to the UK, we continued with our lives. We found teaching posts and within a few years we had a daughter, whom we named Fern Amina. Later, as a family of three, we moved to Tanzania for a couple of years where we worked in an international school.

During our vacations over the years, with our love of wild places, we travelled to mountainous and snowy locations and developed our interests in outdoor pursuits including cross-country skiing and hiking in the mountains.

As the years flew by, Jackie and I maintained an interest in developments in what had once been our home in the Pacific. Having spent those two highly significant years in the Gilbert Islands, we could not forget the bonds and the affection we developed for the islands when we were young adults in our twenties.

These final two chapters are about what has happened in these Pacific islands from the time we left in 1978 until now.

The year after Jackie and I left Beru, the Gilbert Islands became a fully independent nation, the Republic of Kiribati. The word 'Kiribati' is the islanders' spelling and pronunciation of 'Gilberts'.

This new nation is made up of four distinct areas: the Gilbert Islands, Rawaki (formerly the Phoenix Islands), the Line Islands and Banaba Island. A completely new name was chosen for the country that was both modern and encompassed all four areas.

In 2022 the population of the nation totalled more than 123,000 inhabitants. 'Kiribati' is pronounced 'kiree-bass' which unfortunately, is often mispronounced! Some faraway television and radio presenters, don't realise that 'ti' is an 's' in the local language. As a result, the country is often incorrectly referred to as being 'kiree-bar-tee'!

After spending time as the country's chief minister during the 1970s, in July 1979 Ieremia Tabai became the first President of Kiribati. This parliamentary democratic republic has its base on Tarawa, where the elected members initially met in the House of Assembly. However, in the year 2000, a new modern building replaced it and was named *Maneaba ni Maungatabu,* translated as 'the maneaba of the sacred mountain'. Architecturally, both buildings resemble an *I-Kiribati* (meaning Gilbertese) maneaba emphasising the continuing link with the nation's history and traditions.

Although Kiribati only totals 811square kms of actual land, the thirty-three islands making up the nation are located over an incredible 3.5 million square kms of the Pacific Ocean, 3,900kms west to east, 2,100kms from north to south and straddling the Equator. So, where are these four parts of Kiribati in relation to each other?

First of all, there is the archipelago of the sixteen Gilbert Islands, spread over 780kms. The second area is the Rawaki archipelago, consisting of eight islands located 1,600kms to the east of the Gilbert's chain. The third group is 3,000kms even further to the east, the Line Islands. This archipelago runs for 2,350kms northwest to southeast, where Kiribati has sovereignty over eight of the eleven atolls. Finally, the fourth part of Kiribati is Banaba Island, 400kms to the west of the Gilbert Islands. Together, these thirty-three slithers of land within a vast ocean, cover an area equivalent to that of the continental United States! Extraordinary!

Jackie and I just about understood the geography of the Gilbert Islands when we were living there. The most northerly island is Makin then, working southward, there are the islands of Butaritari, Marakei, Abaiang, Tarawa, Maiana, Abemama, Kuria, Aranuka, Nonouti, Tabiteuea, Beru, Nikunau, Onotoa, Tamana and finally Arorae.

These were the islands the adults and pupils at our school talked about mostly, where they visited or had family. Having conversations about these different islands helped us to create a mental picture and understanding of the sixteen atolls. But what about those islands outside the Gilbert Island archipelago?

These island groups, which are also included in Kiribati, are difficult to appreciate and during our two years on Beru we didn't learn much about them. Apart from Banaba, there were very few occasions when the Rawaki or Line Islands were ever referred to. Such huge distances between the different island groups are difficult to comprehend; it's rather like trying to count the mass of stars on one of those clear Pacific night skies!

The Rawaki archipelago includes eight atolls to the east of the Gilbert Islands: Kanton, Enderbury, Rawaki (formerly Phoenix), Manra (formerly Sydney), Bernie, McKean, Nikumaroro (formerly Gardner) and Oromo (formerly Hull).

In 1937 the Phoenix Islands, as they were then called, were incorporated into the Gilbert and Ellice Island Colony by the British. All these atoll islands were uninhabited.

The colonial authorities came up with the 'Phoenix Island Resettlement Scheme' to alleviate overcrowding on some of the Gilbert Island atolls. The aim was to resettle islanders on three of the islands in the group: Orona, Nikumaroro and Manra.

When these settlers from the Gilberts arrived, they were impressed by the number of birds and crabs, and the lagoons full of fish. They planted pandanus, coconut and breadfruit trees, built houses and dug wells.

By 1940, these three islands had a population totalling some 727 settlers but, after a time, certain problems were revealed. A significant difficulty was that the well water was too saline; coupled with prolonged droughts, this resulted in a shortage of fresh water. Also, over time many settlers started missing their relatives and their ancient lands on their original islands. There was a general feeling of isolation, exacerbated by supply ships calling infrequently at Rawaki.

Communication with the outside world was poor and was not helped by the Second World War breaking out after the resettlement scheme had begun when communications and shipping were disrupted across the Pacific region. The challenges on the Rawaki islands were such that by 1963 the resettlement experiment was abandoned.

There is another part to the Rawaki story. In 1938, the United States laid claim to two different atolls in the same archipelago:

Kanton and Enderbury. In 1939, after disagreements between Britain and the United States, the two nations decided to run the islands as a condominium.

A base was constructed on Kanton Island, first as a seaplane landing-site then for aircraft on their long flights across the Pacific from North America to New Zealand. It was seen as a suitable refuelling point and a number of facilities were built on the atoll, including a power station, hotel, medical facilities and a school. These remained until they were no longer required; by 1965, more advanced aircraft could fly longer distances across the Pacific.

Also, between 1960 and 1965 the United States maintained a tracking system on the island as part of their space flight programme.

In 1976, all the facilities on Kanton were abandoned by both the United States and Britain. As a result, most of the workforce left the island and the buildings fell into disrepair. The United States' claims to these two islands were eventually dropped; consequently, in 1979, all the atolls of Rawaki were included within the new nation of Kiribati. By 2015, there were only around twenty individuals still living on Kanton Island.

Interestingly, in 2008 the Kiribati government spearheaded by the then-president, Anote Tong, decided to turn the whole of the Rawaki archipelago into the 'Phoenix Islands Protected Area' (PIPA). It became the world's largest marine protected region and a UNESCO World Heritage site covering an ocean area roughly the size of California, a unique location of both marine and terrestrial habitats. This mid-ocean wilderness, with its submerged volcanoes and eight atolls, was recognised as one of the planet's pristine coral archipelago ecosystems, virtually untouched by humans.

As PIPA pointed out at the time:

The area contains approximately 800 known species of fauna, including 200 coral species, 514 fish species,18 marine mammals and 44 bird species.

All commercial fishing activity was banned from the region to protect its extraordinary natural diversity and in an attempt to secure the world's tuna population in a region where many of the fish lived and were being caught by ships from across the world.

It became an island archipelago of unspoiled ocean wilderness and accompanying land with a massive population of both flora and fauna, an extraordinary natural environment in the middle of the Pacific Ocean!

Unfortunately, and somewhat controversially, PIPA was abandoned in 2021 and the area was opened up to international fishing; the government had decided to increase I-Kiribati revenue by issuing foreign fishing licences. Initially, there was an agreement that Kiribati would be amply compensated for creating this protected zone for nature, but the government felt let down by the lack of financial support. As a consequence, the island nation of Kiribati, which continually struggles to make its way in the world, took the difficult decision to allow commercial fishing into PIPA waters.

As President Taneti Maamau, the next leader of Kiribati, explained:

Similar to any government, our decisions as we make them put the livelihoods of our people at the fore… Our decision as a sovereign country … is to promote the growth of Kiribati's blue economy and uplift the lives of all I-Kiribati.

It was pointed out that Kiribati had lost tens of millions of dollars in revenue by not awarding international fishing licences in the PIPA zone. It couldn't have been an easy decision for the I-Kiribati Government to make.

The Line Islands, far to the east of Rawaki, are also included in the new nation of Kiribati. Eight of the islands in this very long archipelago became part of Kiribati whilst three islands in the chain remain territories of the United States. The Kiribati Line Islands include Teraina (formerly Washington), Tabuaeran (formerly Fanning), Kiritimati (formerly Christmas), Morden, Starbuck, Millennium (formerly Caroline), Vostok and Flint.

Initially Britain took control of three of these islands in 1919 and they were incorporated in the Gilbert and Ellice Islands

Colony. Today these are the only inhabited ones: Kiritimati, Teraina and Tabuaeran.

However, there is evidence of settlements having been on some of these islands as far back as the 1400s. Historians believe that these sites were probably settled by Polynesians as they journeyed across this part of the Pacific Ocean, illustrating the hypothesis that this region was very much the domain of the Polynesian people.

Kiritimati Island has the largest area of any atoll in the world: 388 square kms and 150kms around its perimeter. Incredibly, the island comprises 70% of the entire I-Kiribati land! During the colonial era, coconut plantations and fishing were developed by islanders who settled there from the Gilbert Islands.

During World War Two, Kiritimati Island was a base for the United States and its allies on which an airfield was constructed. After the war, this facility was used for nuclear testing; between 1957 and 1962, the British and Americans carried out thirty-three nuclear bomb tests on Kiritimati Island and nearby Malden Island.

While some military personnel wore protective clothing and goggles, many did not; the islanders (about 260 people at the time) were simply told to leave their homes, turn their backs on the explosion, cover themselves with a blanket and put their hands over their eyes.

When a device was detonated, there was an ear-piercing bang, an intense bright light and a rush of searing heat. Some people were knocked over by the blast and there was damage to buildings. Many trees were snapped in half. Over time, some military personnel and Kiritimati islanders developed significant health problems including cancers, blindness, hearing problems, heart difficulties and reproductive damage.

In 2015, the Kiribati permanent representative to the UN, Ambassador Makurita Baaro, stated:

'Today, our communities still suffer from the long-term impacts of tests, experiencing higher rates of cancer, particularly thyroid cancer, due to exposure to radiation.'

Such ongoing health problems have been challenging; Kiritimati Island only has one small hospital and three small health clinics, facilities inadequate for treating diseases attributed to nuclear testing. Both military personnel and islanders who were subjected to these tests have been studied over the years to establish the amount of damage it caused.

The population of Kiritimati Island in 2020 numbered 7380 residing in three different settlements in the north of the large atoll. London is the main village, where a large modern jetty has been constructed to enable seagoing vessels to visit. The village of Banana is closest to Cassidy International Airport, where schedule planes arrive from both Hawaii and Fiji. Most of the population live in the third Kiritimati village, Tabwakea.

The island's main exports are copra, aquarium fish and seaweed. Although some local fish is eaten, most food is imported. There are primary schools and two high schools on Kiritimati, together with an I-Kiribati technology centre and Hawaiian climatological research facility.

Unlike other I-Kiribati islands, Kiritimati has developed a small tourist industry where visitors can catch fish in its waters. Due to the large population of seabirds on the island, it has also become a wildlife sanctuary.

To the north-west of Kiritimati Island is the unique island of Teraina with its partially filled lagoon. There is a substantial freshwater lake and a large area of peat bog, and canals have been cut into the bog to allow boats to travel between villages. In other areas there is lush vegetation and tall coconut trees.

There is a population of almost 1800 on Teraina in eight villages. Situated between Teraina and Kiritimati is Tabuaeran Island, another atoll where villagers (numbering some 2000 people) live along its western side. On the eastern side, the island has been made into a nature reserve. Cruise ships occasionally call so tourists can sample life on a Pacific island.

Although the Line Islands are a very long way from the capital of the nation on Tarawa, they have become an important facet of present-day Kiribati. In 1994 the I-Kiribati government took the decision to realign the International Dateline so that the entire nation was in the same time zone. This involved moving the I-

Kiribati part of the International Dateline more than 3,000kms eastwards!

The realignment meant that one uninhabited Line Island belonging to Kiribati, Caroline Island, became the first land in the entire world to witness the dawn of the new millennium at the start of 2000.

Kiribati took advantage of this fact in a big way. The island was renamed Millennium Island. Although it was uninhabited, many visitors travelled there to celebrate the first sunrise of the new millennium including about seventy I-Kiribati who would be singing and dancing, behind-the-scene organisers and dignitaries and the I-Kiribati president at the time, Teburoro Tito. There was also a host of foreign journalists and technicians from across the globe.

It was quite a logistical feat to construct a temporary settlement with accommodation and facilities. The sophisticated equipment required for broadcasting was installed on another section of the island.

As dawn broke, the sights and sounds of I-Kiribati singing and dancing against a backdrop of a golden sky were beamed around the world! It was a great opportunity to promote Kiribati as it was, quite literally, placed in the spotlight. Using satellite technology, an estimated audience of one billion enjoyed this extraordinary one-off Pacific performance.

John Simpson of the UK's BBC was amongst those on the island:

Standing here, under the extraordinary, brilliant stars, on a bed of coral, the dancers were singing their hearts out, chanting, beating their great box drums. At the key moment they all shouted Tekeraoi, which means congratulations. There was a real feeling of excitement.

Jackie and I were among the audience, sitting mesmerised in front of our TV in the north of England. As we gazed at the screen, we were transported back to the 1970s, to Beru and our maneaba on Rongorongo. That superb harmonious singing, the swishing of the grass skirts, the clapping, that lone person's chant beginning each dance, the head and arm movements, the colourful outfits, the excitement ... for that special celebration of a new beginning, we were back on our island. The sights and sounds awakened memories and, as the I-Kiribati sang and danced, we were in a mixed-up zone of past and future. The power of television! The magic of Kiribati!

The fourth part of this new nation of Kiribati, is Banaba Island (previously called Ocean Island), 400kms to the west of the Gilbert Island archipelago. Uniquely amongst the thirty-three islands of Kiribati, Banaba is a raised atoll and the only island with some height, with the highest point in all Kiribati at 87m!

Similar to the island of Nauru, during ancient times it was a favourite location for thousands of migrating seabirds that deposited deep thicknesses of their droppings. This guano eventually transformed into high-grade phosphate some 12m thick.

Over the centuries Pacific travellers occasionally arrived on the island, and seafarers from Melanesia to the southeast and nearby Kiribati to the west made Banaba their home. The indigenous inhabitants of Banaba spoke I-Kiribati.

These settlers followed a life of subsistence, producing their own food and fishing. They grew a range of edible vegetables on the fertile land and found an abundance of marine life.

On the island of Banaba, with a circumference of a mere 10kms, there is no surface water and this can be a problem in times of drought. But quite unique to Banaba is the fresh water obtained from caves beneath the island, known as *te bangabanga*.

In 1900, Britain annexed Banaba, at which point those living on the island had their lives changed abruptly. The Pacific Islands Company started mining phosphate on the island around the same time. This prized rock was used for fertiliser and was gradually taken away from the island by ship and transported mainly to Australia and New Zealand.

The workforce included Banabans, Chinese and some I-Kiribati, and was overseen by Australian and British managers. A purpose-built, narrow-gauge railway was built and huge cantilevers constructed to load the phosphate onto ships; it was a systematic process of stripping the surface layer off the island and taking it away.

During the Second World War, Banaba Island was invaded by the Japanese between 1942 and 1945. Europeans and Chinese workers involved with phosphate mining were evacuated before their arrival, but some of the Banabans and I-Kiribati were taken to Japanese forced-labour camps on faraway islands.

However, 150 islanders were kept on the island at the mercy of their captors. They were forced to fish for the troops, provide them with other food and carry out a range of additional tasks. They experienced much ill-treatment by the Japanese: some were murdered; there were regular beatings; others were tortured; women were raped, and most suffered from malnutrition.

As the war drew to a close, to stop anybody giving testimony against the Japanese invaders, the soldiers decided to massacre all the islanders who remained on Banaba. Their wrists were tied, they were blindfolded and ordered to sit at the edge of a cliff facing out to sea. Soldiers with bayonets stabbed them in the back and kicked them off the cliff. As they lay on rocks or in the water below, the Japanese shot them.

One man, Kabunare Koura, miraculously survived this mass killing – remarkably, he wasn't severely stabbed or shot! As his fellow islanders lay dead at the bottom of the cliff, he stayed as still as he could and pretended to be dead. After nightfall, he made his escape.

For almost two months, he hid in caves and among the island's rock pinnacles. When he saw that Australian soldiers had arrived, he tentatively made his way to the centre of the island. He was safe! Fortunately, he was able to provide testimony and those Japanese military in charge on Banaba were charged with war crimes.

Unfortunately, after the war Banaban islanders were not allowed back on their island; the British colonial authorities claimed that all their houses had been destroyed. Instead, the Banabans and I-Kiribati from the Japanese labour camps, numbering more than 1000, were relocated some 2,100kms south-east to the Fijian island of Rabi. The British had previously purchased the island for this very purpose and the Banabans were informed that Rabi would now be their home!

Although this new island was considerably larger than Banaba, it was an alien environment with unusual vegetation, undulating land, different fish in the sea, cows grazing and limited fresh water.

Meanwhile, expatriates continued to mine phosphate back on Banaba. Over many years, more than 300 Banabans eventually managed to return to their island. Mining continued until the phosphate was depleted in 1979, by which time 90% of the island's original surface had been stripped away.

Since their arrival on Rabi, the Banaban and I-Kiribati islanders have adapted to life in Fiji, but the people of Rabi have become a political anomaly. After the independence of Kiribati in 1979, although residing in Fiji these islanders have I-Kiribati passports. On Rabi, they control their own affairs and have their own council, and they are allowed to send a representative to the Kiribati Parliament. Quite extraordinarily, in 2005 the Fijian Government also gave all Rabi islanders Fijian citizenship – but most of them still consider Banaba to be their spiritual home.

Present-day Banaba is a challenging place to live. After decades of phosphate mining, nearly all the vegetation has been destroyed including coconut, pandanus and other trees essential for island living. The islanders struggle to grow crops as Banaba suffers from regular, lengthy droughts. As there is little fresh water on the island, over recent years it has become reliant on a small desalination plant but when that breaks down the islanders struggle to survive.

Before mining took place, people found fresh water in the ancient te bangabanga caves beneath Banaba. Unfortunately these are now contaminated because of years of mining and Banabans have suffered a variety of health problems through drinking unclean water.

Many islanders now show symptoms of malnourishment. There is a lack of medical support on the island and when emergencies occur communications are problematic. Supply ships from Tarawa only appear every few months.

Katerina Teaiwa, of the Australian National University and of Banaban heritage, has commented on the impact of phosphate mining on her ancestral home.

She has said:

'They came, had a big party, made lots of money and left.'

Many people have been shocked at the injustice suffered by the inhabitants of this speck of a raised atoll in the middle of the ocean. Some compensation was eventually awarded by the British for the way the Banabans were treated and their island decimated.

The island's ability to successfully sustain the original numbers of Banabans is nigh-on impossible, given the array of environmental concerns. The Banaban elders living on Rabi have fought the I-Kiribati government for a greater share of the millions of dollars trust money from phosphate mining. The residents have suggested that Banaba cede from Kiribati and be taken over by Fiji . There have even been calls for Banaba to become an independent nation similar to its near neighbour, Nauru, which also suffered from years of phosphate mining. But whatever the future brings, those Banabans residing on their island are determined to remain, however challenging their lives become.

So there we have the four island areas which make up the Republic of Kiribati. Many references, documents, reports and books, many of which are online, outline the present-day situation of this new nation. There is no doubt that the remoteness and scattered nature of its thirty-three islands has its challenges.

Covering such a huge part of the Pacific Ocean, there continue to be shipping and communication problems. Economic factors essential for the success of I-Kiribati finances include: continued foreign government aid, for example from Australia and New Zealand; revenue from foreign government fishing licences in Kiribati waters; ongoing copra production; and, overseas worker remittances from those working across the world, especially aboard foreign ships.

Fortunately for Kiribati, the nation sits within a 360,000,000-square-kilometre economic zone, a much larger area than any other in the region. Granting fishing licences in I-Kiribati waters in 2016 accounted for around 75% of the nation's national income. In recent years, licences have been granted to South Korea, Japan, China, the European Union and the United States. More tuna is caught in I-Kiribati waters than any other fishing area in the world!

About half the population of Kiribati now live on South Tarawa, and this has brought about the most pressing list of concerns for the nation. So many islanders living side by side on the main island with polluted drinking water and poor sanitation has resulted in an increase in diarrhoeal diseases.

Building causeways across many of the islets has altered the natural regeneration of Tarawa's lagoon, resulting in ecological damage. Equally, the island has become polluted with discarded human detritus including tin cans, plastic items and old vehicles.

Like the world over, there is a desire for material items but what to do with them when they are no longer of use is a major problem. There are areas of Tarawa where refuse is piled high.

An additional challenge has been the move away from a subsistence way of life on the main island because of the number of people. With so many new inhabitants, it is not possible to carry out traditional practices. This has led to the consumption of more imported food which, in turn, has resulted in an increase in obesity and diabetes.

There are further facets of a changing world within Kiribati. In his book, *A History of Kiribati*, Walsh writes that on South Tarawa in 2016:

41% of households in South Tarawa had a desktop or laptop computer, 25% had a tablet computer, and 29% had a television (used for watching video films as there is no indigenous TV service).

We all want access to the technological revolution, and why not? But how can Kiribati enjoy the benefits of the modern world and retain a healthy lifestyle and not destroy its unique island environment? These are all significant concerns for I-Kiribati society today and for the future.

Over the years, the government's aim has been to guide the I-Kiribati people through this ever-changing world. However, isolation and limited resources still appear to hamper the development of this island nation. The mainstay of life, especially on islands away from Tarawa, continues to be one of subsistence fishing and farming. The I-Kiribati still fish around their islands, both on shore and in canoes, to feed their families. They continue to cut karewe from coconut trees and consume traditional food. The flow of life we became familiar with during our life on Beru appears to be mostly alive and well.

Two Italians who visited the islands in 2016 wrote a book simply entitled *Kiribati*. Alice Piciocchi and Andrea Angeli found islands with:

Magical rites, legends, customs linked to the landscape and its resources, rhythms determined by the tides, community and social relationships, behaviours, artefacts, symbols, values and cultural conventions...

These are similar to our own experiences during the 1970s. Alongside such age-old island traditions, since independence the government has worked within the modern world. Despite the island nation continuing a subsistence way of life together with its other sources of income, Kiribati remains one of the least developed countries in the world.

But life in Kiribati after independence continues in its own individual way. As the authors of *Kiribati – Aspects of History* put it:

Our independence is only meaningful to us [when] we have it in our own Gilbertese way, 'te Katie ni Kiribati'.... We have arrived at the present, changed, but strong in our sense of Gilbertese identity.

What happens to Kiribati in the future will very much depend on what takes place over the coming years. Indeed, the immediate future is going to be critical for I-Kiribati society and for Kiribati as a nation.

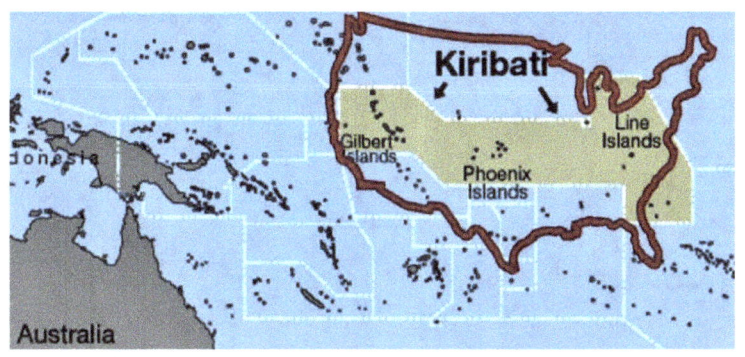

Kiribati compared with the size of continental USA

The Kiribati flag

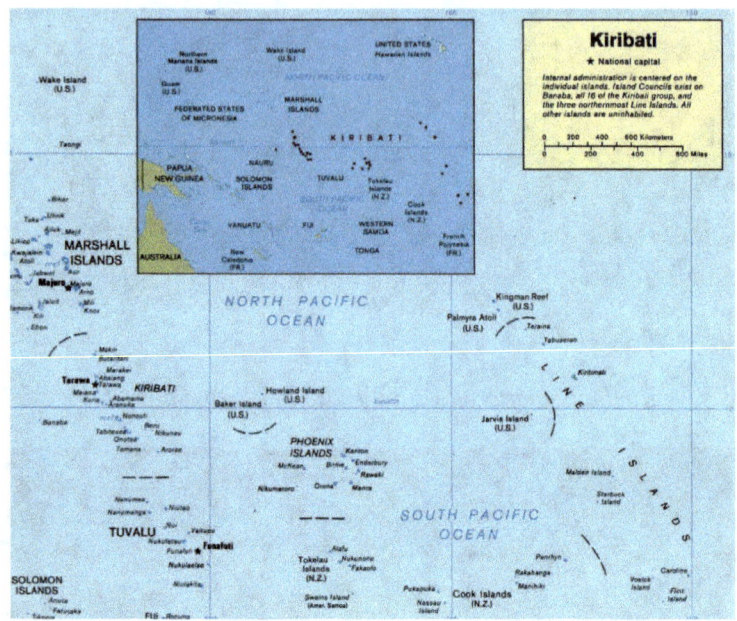

The Map of Kiribati

Chapter 18

The Rising Tides of Beru

There is a major phenomenon that is threatening the future of Kiribati: global warming. The recent increase in temperature of planet Earth could result in the eventual demise of this low-lying island nation.

Scientists agree that during the last decade the sea level has risen on average 3.6mms every year. In Kiribati, the sea level has risen between 21cms and 24cms since 1880, with a third of that rise occurring in the last twenty-five years. If this continues, Kiribati could well be covered by water and uninhabitable by the year 2100.

Such predictions have alarming consequences for I-Kiribati people, their way of life and their culture. The former president of Kiribati, Anote Tong, sums up the concerns of the nation:

For us climate change is not an event in the future. It's an event that we're dealing with now ... our entire survival is at stake.

The Earth's climate has often experienced periods of change over the centuries. There have been fluctuations in our climate due to natural factors within the environment, such as the Ice Ages or when there has been intense volcanic activity. However, the increase in global temperatures during recent decades has been caused mainly by human activity. The burning of coal, oil and gas in manufacturing processes and transportation, together with cutting down forests, have contributed to rising global temperatures by producing more greenhouse gases such as carbon dioxide and methane. Once in the atmosphere, these gases have helped to trap in heat, which has led to rising global temperatures. This has resulted in a measurable increase in the warming of the atmosphere, land and oceans.

Scientists have plotted the rise in the warming of the planet since the pre-industrial period. From 1880 to 1981, the average rise was 0.08°C, but in the last forty years it has risen by 0.18°C. It is predicted that the average temperature could rise to 1.5°C in the next twenty years! After a report by the Intergovernmental Panel on Climate Change (IPCC) in 2021, Antonio Guterres, the UN Secretary-General proclaimed:

Today's IPCC Report is a code red for humanity. The alarm bells are deafening, and the evidence is irrefutable: greenhouse gas emissions from fossil fuel burning and deforestation are choking our planet and putting billions of people at immediate risk.

Such rises in temperature across the world have resulted in significant challenges for our planet. In some regions, they have given rise to more volatile weather with more frequent storms, flooding, droughts, water shortages and wildfires. There are regions of the planet where deserts have expanded or where crops are failing due to changed weather patterns, leading to food shortages.

The areas of our planet which reveal striking evidence of climate change are in the Arctic and Antarctic. Both polar regions are important temperature regulators for the planet, where snow and ice reflect heat back into space. With reduced snow and ice, the amount of reflected heat becomes less thus helping temperatures to rise.

In the Arctic, sea ice has reduced by 13% per decade over the last thirty years; similarly, the Antarctic has experienced rising temperatures which have resulted in an increase in melting ice. That extra meltwater ends up in the seas and oceans, allowing sea levels to rise.

As well as melting polar ice, glaciers in the high mountains have similarly been affected by rising global temperatures. In the Northern Hemisphere alone, 85% of the glaciers retreated between the years 2000 and 2020. An incredible 509 smaller glaciers worldwide have simply disappeared! Having visited mountainous locations most of my life, I have witnessed how global warming has affected such regions. In the European Alps, it is possible to see evidence of retreating glaciers simply by looking at the amount of moraine (the rocks, gravel and sand) that has been left behind as a glacier has slowly shrunk. Such examples include the Mer de Glacé in the French Alps, which has retreated around two kilometres since 1850. Every year over the past few decades, this French glacier has lost between three and five metres from its snout. Then there is the Gorner Glacier in the Swiss Alps, which is now about three kilometres shorter than it was during the mid-1800s!

There are many, many examples of shrinking glaciers within other high mountain regions around the world in the Himalaya, Andes, Rockies, Southern Alps and East African Mountains.

One of the delights of walking upon glacier ice in the summer months is to watch the streams of water flowing upon its icy surface. Such meltwater, as it gurgles and bounces along on top of the ice, will flow out of the glacier and eventually reach the sea and add to the rising ocean level. The European Geoscience Union warns us that more than 90% of glacier volume could be lost by 2100!

As if this were not alarming enough, due to the thermal expansion of water as global temperatures increase, the level of the oceans will rise yet further. Experiments easily illustrate how water expands when heated. This, in terms of our oceans, will increase the volume of sea water as global temperatures rise. As the planet warms up, surface ice will melt and the heating of that water will expand further, simply because of the increase in global heating.

If rising sea level predictions are correct, if nothing is done to slow down the warming of our planet, many nations across the globe will become vulnerable to flooding. In 2021 it was calculated that 267 million people worldwide live less than two metres above sea level. By the year 2100, the rise in sea level is estimated to be at least 0.3m, but in the worst-case scenario as much as 2.5m! This will result in many coastland areas, including numerous major cities across the world, becoming increasingly threatened by rising waters. If this becomes a reality, experts predict that the cities of Tokyo, Shanghai, Dhaka, Kolkata, Miami, Alexandria, Mumbai and numerous others may be in danger of being lost to rising sea levels.

Presumably, if such rises occur, coastline defences could be constructed and vulnerable populations relocated to higher ground. But what happens if your nation does not have any land above those predicted levels of 2.5m? Sadly, this is the case for the Pacific Ocean low-lying island nations such as the Marshall Islands, Tuvalu and, of course, Kiribati.

As Anote Tong has stated, *'It's an event that we're dealing with now.'* Indeed, over the past years, Kiribati, has had to contend with an array of challenges directly related to global warming. Atolls are facing rising sea levels which have led to numerous reports of the effects they have had on I-Kiribati life.

In Tarawa, the capital, where around half of the population of Kiribati now live, abnormally high tides – 'king tides' – now regularly cover the land. During the 1970s when we lived on Beru, there were high tides but never ones that flooded great swathes of the island, including villages.

Another recent phenomenon related to changes in our climate is that major storms are developing closer to the islands and causing storm surges on some of the atolls. Sea water has swamped homes, maneabas and other buildings, and people have been devastated by the destruction the flooding leaves behind. Some islanders have moved their homes to areas less prone to flooding, but relocating is extremely challenging when the highest point is mainly less than three metres above sea level!

In an overcrowded area like South Tarawa where more than 63,000 people live, moving to a more suitable site isn't really an option. The residents live on small plots of land covering just 10^2kms of the atoll, so it's simply a matter of drying out their dwellings, cleaning up and carrying on with their lives – until the next time!

One temporary measure islanders have been experimenting with in an attempt to hold back the destructive nature of the water is building sea walls using coral rock found on the atolls. These defensive constructions have had varying levels of success depending on how high and forceful the high tides have been.

Over time some sea walls have been modified and built even higher as the sea continues to batter them. Fortunate residents who manage to acquire cement can make the wall stronger by bonding the rocks together or buildings walls of concrete. Unfortunately this is only a temporary measure and little match for a determined sea surge or king tide.

Another weapon in the fight against the rising sea level is planting mangrove trees. The strong roots of these tropical trees help protect the shores from coastal erosion by binding the sand together. In addition, mangroves can act as buffers during powerful storm surges; they also provide habitats for fish and crabs, thus adding creatures to the local ecosystem. Planting mangroves is a straightforward process that requires no sophisticated equipment; holes can be made into the sand where mangrove seeds are planted and this can be done easily by islanders. In just a few weeks, young mangrove trees will be growing.

With average tides steadily increasing, the freshwater lens beneath the atolls is altered and the freshwater within the lens might be diminished. This is extremely serious because people rely on wells that tap into the lens that occur naturally beneath atolls. Well-water is used for drinking, cooking and watering crops; with rising sea levels, the zone where wells once extracted freshwater might become increasingly brackish. Only wells at the centre of islands, where the lens is at its deepest, might be suitable for use.

A study carried out in 2019 on how rising sea level has impacted on underground freshwater concurred that salt water intrusion in the South Tarawa area did have an effect on the quality and quantity of the freshwater lens. Any damage to the freshwater lens beneath atolls might take considerable time to recover. Furthermore, with sea water flooding the normally dry land, crops might significantly reduce their growth and quality because soil salinity can reduce a crop's yield. The World Health Organisation warned of other problems:

In Kiribati, climate change is expected to increase the risk of infectious and vector-borne diseases, particularly dengue fever, diarrhoeal disease, and cholera. Populated areas such as Tarawa, may be most heavily impacted.

The rise in sea temperatures has resulted in some coral bleaching, where stressed microscopic algae residing within corals no longer live. Corals are strongholds of biodiverse ecosystems and they act as natural barriers that absorb the force of waves and storm surges. If bleaching continues, coral growth and reproductivity will be hindered and inevitably lead to their death.

Tabea Lissner et al, in the book *Climate Change Adaptation in Pacific Countries*, concludes:

Coral reefs are of central importance for islands ... [including] ... buffering functions against storm impacts and coastal erosion ... ocean acidification as a consequence of increased uptake of CO_2, presents a major threat to the calcification of corals. Increasing water temperatures can lead to coral bleaching...

A great deal of research and reporting about the consequences of global warming has been carried out on the island of Tarawa; after all, it is the nation's capital and facilities exist for completing such investigations. However, you can imagine my delight when I came across, *Kiribati – Beru Island Strategic Plan 2021–2024*.

This is a 2020 Kiribati Government document sponsored by a number of organisations to establish the effects of global warming upon a selection of outer islands. Amazingly, one of those islands was Beru!

Heatwaves, seawater inundation caused by king tides, drought, coastal erosion, strong winds and seawater inundation caused by sea surges were the main features from the previous three years. Beru locations where such climatic problems had occurred were photographed and mapped. There was evidence of flooding at various locations, evidence of coastal erosion and a collapsed causeway at the village of Teteirio. We often cycled across that causeway as VSOs!

The maps show where the highest tides were encroaching on the beaches; it was shocking to see that they were flooding many buildings in villages and becoming a regular occurrence in Nuka, Aoniman, Taboiaki and Eriko. These were people's homes on land where they would have planted vegetables, cut karewe and kept chickens and pigs. It must be quite devastating when such flooding takes place.

The big question is: what can Kiribati do to try to halt the rise in sea levels apart from constructing walls and planting mangrove trees in vulnerable areas of coastline?

When Anote Tong was elected as the new Kiribati President in 2003, he made the problem of rising waters around his country a priority. Wherever he travelled, both home and abroad, he asked pertinent questions about what should be done. After all, in 2020 Kiribati was only responsible for 0.52 tonnes of CO_2 emissions whereas more developed countries, such as the United States, were producing 13.68 tonnes. Tong argued that although Kiribati had little to do with causing the problem, it was suffering the most. It was a question of fairness.

In Kiribati, people cannot migrate to a new location away from rising sea levels because there is no higher land to flee to. However, Tong got to work on what seemed an insurmountable task.

After considerable deliberation, in 2014 he purchased some land on Vanua Levu on the island in Fiji, around 2000 kilometres from Kiribati. The land was on the Natovato Estate owned by the Anglican Church and had been a sanctuary for ethnic Solomon Islanders, who were descendants of slaves within the Pacific region, since the late 1800s. Part of the purchase deal was that a section of the estate would be kept aside for the Solomon Islanders. Then, if and when some members of the I-Kiribati community wished to settle in Fiji, they would have somewhere to escape to.

The Tong purchase wasn't without its critics and some said it would be difficult for I-Kiribati to adjust to living in a high-island environment; others said that the purchase of the Fijian land was too expensive at US$ 8.77 million.

President Tong explained:

We would hope not to put everyone on one piece of land, but if it became absolutely necessary, yes, we could do it... It's basically a matter of survival.

During his tenure as president of Kiribati, he made it his mission to plead with world leaders to reduce carbon dioxide emissions. He raised awareness of the desperate situation of atoll nations and even suggested to New Zealand and Australia, that migrants from Kiribati could re-settle in their countries. Tong referred to such a move as 'migration with dignity', where I-Kiribati would be specifically trained for particular jobs, ready for integration into a new nation. As a consequence, New Zealand has been allowing 75 I-Kiribati per year to move to their country.

There have been a number of more ambitious proposals to solve the Kiribati problem of rising sea levels, one of which was to build floating islands for the inhabitants. A detailed model of small pentagonal-shaped platforms that could be connected together was designed as part of an international 'Kiribati Floating Housing' competition. Each platform could hold five houses for as many as 30 people and include a greenhouse, water purification system, vegetable garden and solar panels. The winner of the competition was Polish architect Martin Kitala. However, with a cost for its construction of more than $2 billion, as yet it has not been developed.

There have been other ambitious designs for floating dwellings but they remain ideas on computer screens; the cost of such projects is a major factor in them not receiving the go ahead.

Another suggestion is to use massive dredgers to raise the height of atolls. Calculations have suggested that raising the islands by just 1–1.5m, would be enough to secure an island's safety for fifty years or more.

President Maamau, who took over from Anote Tong, looked at a number of solutions to solve the Kiribati sea-level problem. He wasn't keen on the migration strategy, which would force citizens to leave their ancestral homes, and neither did he endorse *'the misleading and pessimistic scenario of a sinking, deserted nation'* as he described it. Instead he preferred the use of massive dredgers to raise the height of islands.

Engineering specialists have suggested that the proposal was feasible but islanders would have to be temporally relocated while the work took place. Sand and gravel could be dredged from the lagoon to raise the height of the land. The scheme is not without its critics; some experts warn that such dredging would seriously impact on the coral reef population and marine ecosystem.

Other ideas to save Kiribati from the rising ocean include: constructing major sea defences around atolls; shipping tonnes of earth to the islands in order to raise atoll elevations; constructing a platform over each atoll which could then be built upon, and raising every building in a village onto stilts – but exactly what to do is still being debated.

Anote Tong and Akka Rimon wrote at the end of November of 2021, just after COP 26, the International Climate Conference meeting in Glasgow:

Are we scared? Of course. We are in the front line of this crisis, despite having done amongst the least to cause it. It is difficult to leave the only home we have known. But science does not lie. And we can see the water coming… But it will take the global village to save our small village and keep alive our culture, language, heritage, spirits, land, waters and above all, our people.

It is imperative that such words from these Pacific islands are listened to and acted upon. For too many decades there have been warnings about the impending catastrophe if we don't ward off these threats to our planet. Since the 1960s, the cries have steadily increased about halting the amount of greenhouse gases being pumped into the atmosphere, but the huge effort required for the world to change has not been taking place.

I agree with former US President Barack Obama when he said:

'We are the first generation to feel the effect of climate change and the last generation who can do something about it.'

Let us hope that future international environmental agreements can be maintained and become a priority for every nation so we can stem the tide of inaction in order to stem the increase in rising sea tides around our planet!

To end, here are two further quotes from different islanders from those I-Kiribati video clips, similar to the ones cited in the introduction of this book. One young man on Tarawa proudly claimed as he planted mangrove seeds into the sand:

'I just don't want to see my island get drowned under the sea. This is where we belong, this is our identity, this is our culture, this is where our hearts belong.'

And finally, a teenage girl living on Tarawa simply explained with eyes full of tears:

'I don't want Kiribati to disappear!'

These are desperate reflections that ought to stir the humanity in us all.

Jackie and I, who once lived on the islands, stand with the I-Kiribati in wanting to save their nation. We wish to add our voices in solidarity with the islanders we lived with many decades ago. We too wish to keep alive the *'culture, language, heritage, spirits, land, waters and above all, the people'* within these unique Pacific islands.

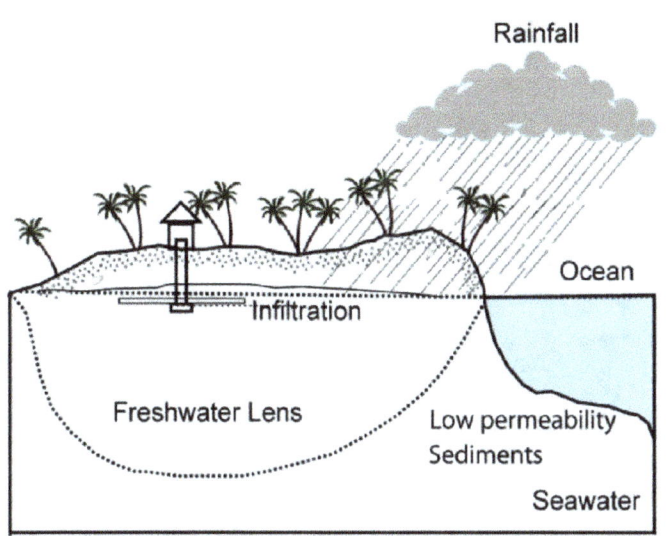

A diagram illustrating the 'fresh water lens' beneath atolls. Underneath the islands, freshwater rests on top of seawater allowing islanders to obtain drinking water.

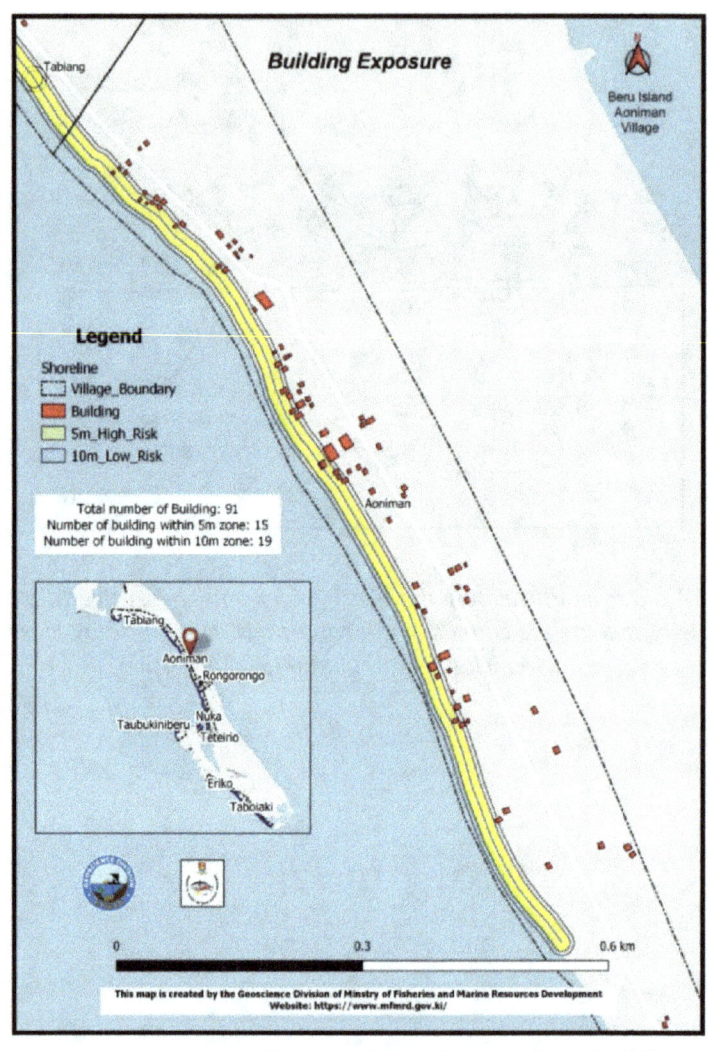

*A map of Aoniman village on Beru showing those buildings which are vulnerable to flooding
Courtesy: Kiribati Government*

A sign pointing out the highest point on Tarawa

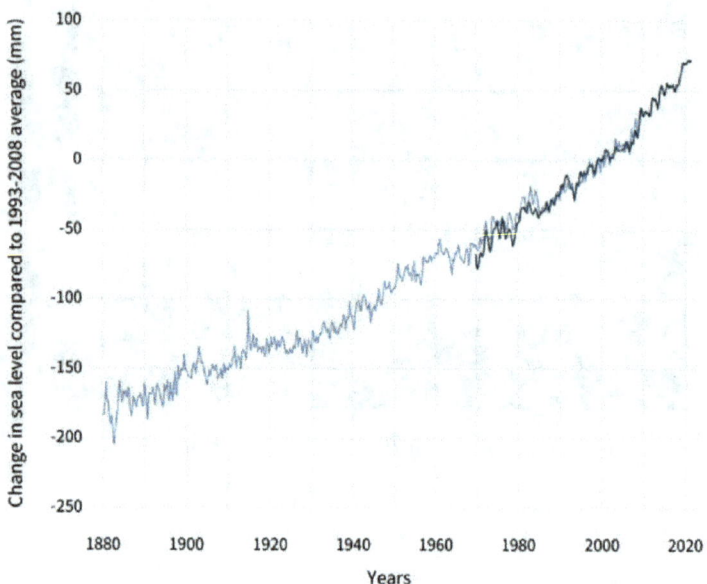

Global sea level rise since 1880
Courtesy: University of Hawaii Sea Level Center

The result of rising sea levels in Kiribati
Courtesy: UNICEF Australia Simon Nazer

The disappearance of glaciers in the Swiss Alps

The vulnerability of Beru due to the rising tides – it is just two or three metres above sea level!

Regular flooding disrupts life in villages in Kiribati
Courtesy: UNICEF Australia Simon Nazer

When the king tides appear, houses are regularly flooded
Courtesy: UNICEF Australia Claire Anterea

When children play in the king tides on Tarawa they are in danger of catching waterborne diseases and diarrhoea.
Courtesy: UNICEF Australia Simon Nazer

Some Suggestions For Further Reading

C. A. Small, *Atoll Agriculture in The Gilbert And Ellice Islands*

Ed. Walter Leal Filho, *Climate Change Adaptation in Pacific Countries*

H. E. Maude, *The Evolution of the Gilbertese Boti*

Tarawa Teachers' College, *The Gilbert and Ellice Islands Colony*

Michael Ravell Walsh, *A History of Kiribati*

Alice Piciocchi and Andrea Angeli, *Kiribati*

Sister Alaima Talu et al, *Kiribati – Aspects of History*

J P Wilkinson, *Letters from a VSO*

Sir Arthur Grimble, arranged and illustrated by Rosemary Grimble, *Migration, Myth and Magic from the Gilbert Islands*

Dick Bird, *Never the Same Again: A History of VSO*

Arthur Grimble, *A Pattern of Islands*

Robert Sherrod, *Tarawa – the Story of a Battle*

David Lewis, *We, the Navigators*

June Knox-Mawer and Peter Carmichael, *A World of Islands*